thenext CMO

A GUIDE TO OPERATIONAL MARKETING EXCELLENCE

SECOND EDITION

PETER **MAHONEY**, SCOTT **TODARO**, DAN **FAULKNER**

ARCHWAY
PUBLISHING

Archway Publishing books may be ordered through booksellers or by contacting:

Archway Publishing
1663 Liberty Drive
Bloomington, IN 47403
www.archwaypublishing.com
844-669-3957

ISBN: 978-1-6657-1139-5 (sc)
ISBN: 978-1-6657-1138-8 (hc)
ISBN: 978-1-6657-1137-1 (e)

Library of Congress Control Number: 2021917450

Print information available on the last page.

Archway Publishing rev. date: 09/08/2021

CONTENTS

ABOUT THE AUTHORS

Peter Mahoney

Peter Mahoney is the founder and CEO of Plannuh, a venture-backed software company providing the first AI-driven platform to automate marketing leadership. Before founding Plannuh, Peter spent more than 30 years as a marketing and product executive with experience as a CMO for startups through multi-billion dollar public companies, including voice and AI leader, Nuance Communications. Peter is also an active board member, angel investor, advisor, a sought-after public speaker, and the host of The Next CMO podcast. Peter has a large following on Twitter via his @nerdCMO account. Peter graduated from Boston College with a double major in Physics and Computer Science and still lives a stone's throw away from campus with his wife and three adultish children.

Scott Todaro

With a passion for marketing, Scott has devoted his 28-year professional career to perfecting the craft. As CMO and co-founder of Plannuh, along with Peter and Dan, Scott is committed to improving the marketing profession by creating a software platform to help marketers optimize their strategies, plans, and budgets. Scott has held marketing leadership positions with seven companies, 4 resulting in successful exits, and has managed hundreds of marketing professionals. In addition to his professional experience, Scott holds BBA and MBA degrees with concentrations in marketing and was an adjunct professor for 4 years at the University of Massachusetts, Lowell teaching marketing strategy to MBA students. Scott lives outside of Boston with his wife Maureen and family. Follow Scott on Twitter @stodaro24.

Dan Faulkner

Dan Faulkner is the CTO of Plannuh, where he is responsible for the technical strategy and delivery of the world's first AI-powered marketing management platform. Dan has 25 years of high-tech experience, spanning research and development, product management, strategy, and general management. He has deep international experience, having led businesses in Europe, Asia, North America, and South America, delivering complex AI solutions at scale to numerous industries. Dan holds a Bachelor's degree in Linguistics, a Masters degree in Speech & Language Processing, and a Masters degree in Marketing. He has completed studies in Strategy Implementation at Wharton. Dan lives in Andover, Massachusetts with his wife and two children.

FOREWORD

The next CMO. That is to say, the next generation of CMOs. I know them well. I talk to them all the time. I've been lucky to work with a handful of future CMOs on my teams at Drift and Privy. And through DGMG I hear from them every day, whether that's in the DGMG community, my podcast, or even just comments on LinkedIn.

There are the students, just learning the ropes and trying to get their foot in the door.

There are the young marketers, fresh out of school, trying to find their place in the marketing world.

The established marketers, with a few years of experience under their belt, are looking for a boost that will get them up to the C-suite. And even current CMOs, who have scaled the marketing mountain and want to stay on top of their game.

But independent of their skill set and expertise, they all have one thing in common: none of them went to school for B2B marketing.

Regardless of age or experience, everyone who shows up on my site comes seeking those magic marketing secrets and systems that can't be read in a book or conveyed in a 20-minute PowerPoint presentation at an all-hands meeting. The kind of knowledge that can only be learned after years of testing, failing, re-testing, then failing again. Things like: How to plan, select a strategy, build a budget, and set and execute on goals. What channels to pursue and which to ignore.

It's stuff that every rising marketer has to grapple with at some point. I remember a younger, more naive Dave Gerhardt saying that he was only going to run marketing plays that his customers loved. Forget about demand generation. Forget about goal setting. It's all about the brand and creating memorable experiences. That made for good clickbait, sure, but it's far from the pro-level operating system you need to run a marketing machine today for a high-growth business today.

And while I'm still an unabashed brand builder (and will defend that position until the day I die), it's a lot easier to only focus on brand plays when you aren't the one who owns the marketing number. Once you're in that leadership position, the cold, hard fact of marketing comes into focus: it's all about driving revenue and growth.

That doesn't mean that you need to abandon brand building entirely and only focus on what generates instant ROI. On the contrary, brand-centric channels like social media, podcasting, YouTube, etc. can be great long-term growth drivers. It just means that you need to understand the business impact of all of your marketing activities.

What is the "why" of everything that you do in marketing?

What's the strategic intent of increasing your social following, doubling your podcast downloads, or investing in your blog?

Great, you have a marketing plan. Now how are you going to execute? What are your guardrails?

These aren't easy questions to answer. Heck, I still deal with some of these challenges on a daily basis, 10+ years into my marketing career. But they are questions that you need to think about and work through if you want to advance up the marketing ladder.

That's why I have so much respect for the whole Plannuh team. Because there is no set OPERATING SYSTEM for modern marketers today. What Peter, Scott, and Dan have done is finally provide some long sought-after answers to those marketing FAQs. They've managed to blend the operational side of marketing with the creative side to help you build a brand that is in service of revenue, not working against your business objectives. This book will give you the insights, templates, models, etc. that you need to implement a strategy that works for YOU and YOUR business, no one else's.

I don't know why I'm still selling it; you already own the book, and you know how good these guys are. Enough from me, the really good stuff starts on the next page. End of foreword.

- Dave Gerhardt

INTRODUCTION

Early in 2020 - right at the time we were all starting to ponder whether the pandemic might impact our businesses - we were finishing up content for the first edition of *The Next CMO*.

We have been "operational marketing advocates" for our entire careers and were excited about the content, but didn't know if we were writing for a small group of fellow operational marketing geeks, or an entire profession that was grappling with massive change and increased fiscal and operational scrutiny.

But with over 10,000 books in circulation in less than a year, the enthusiastic response to our first edition made it clear that we were addressing a broad and accelerating shift in the way the marketing function was managed. And like telehealth, remote working, and digital transformation, the operational marketing movement started with a groundswell but shifted into hyperspeed when the pandemic forced us all to rethink our entire marketing plans in the space of a few short weeks.

The "Great Replan of 2020" made it clearer than ever that strong operational practices translate to agile organizations. These nimble teams can change their approach, maintain focus on their goals, and reprioritize resources to emphasize their highest-return campaigns, while shifting resources away from the money losers. And whether the pandemic drove massive cost reductions or massive growth, operationally-strong marketing teams fared much better than their less operationally-disciplined peers.

We are incredibly excited about this new, expanded edition of *The Next CMO*. We had the opportunity to expand on popular topics like campaign planning and ROI measurement, and we have added new content including:

- How to present marketing results to the board and CEO
- Defining, selecting, and applying marketing strategies
- The growing need for marketing campaign managers
- Statistics from the *Operational Marketing Index* to help you benchmark your level of operational marketing excellence
- More best practices and templates to help structure your strategic and operational marketing

We consistently hear from our readers that they really appreciate the templates and tools that we included in the book. With that in mind, we have expanded the templates and have made them available in digital format on TheNextCMO.com for easy access and download.

Whether you are new to *The Next CMO* or a returning reader, we are confident that our second edition's expanded content will enable you and your team to step up your game as operationally-excellent marketers.

Peter, Scott, and Dan

CHAPTER 1

The Problem with Operational Marketing Leadership

Warning: There is some tough love in this chapter.

It is widely understood that CMOs suffer some of the highest turnover rates in the C-suite. How can that be, given the fact that marketing executives who reach the top rank in the profession have spent years honing their ability to communicate the value of their products and services?

The fundamental problem is that marketing has become increasingly complex over the last two decades, and at the same time, the expectations for effective execution and accurate measurement of marketing functions have grown significantly. And while most marketers have implemented automation systems for delivering and measuring the tactics of marketing, the more strategic issues (including building, measuring, and optimizing the overall marketing plan) are managed manually. As a result, the processes for managing the overall marketing function often buckle as the complexity grows, causing ineffective strategic execution and the inability to clearly demonstrate the value of the marketing function.

The *Harvard Business Review (HBR)* covered this topic extensively and proposed some recommendations in a 2017 report called "The Trouble with CMOs." It offers some solid recommendations to remediate this issue, including aligning expectations and finding the right skills match for the CMO role. But those suggestions don't address the underlying strategic execution problem.

When you look at the results of the "Forrester SiriusDecisions 2019 Global CMO Study," it is clear that CMOs themselves know what needs to improve based on their self-identified areas of focus including:

- Marketing Strategy & Investment
- Marketing Planning & Campaign Strategy
- Transformation
- Marketing Value
- Marketing Organization Design & Development

In short, CMOs agree that their main focus should be defining and executing strategy while proving the value of marketing. Unfortunately, CMOs struggle with both strategic alignment and measuring the true return created from marketing budget allocation.

The Fundamental Responsibilities of the CMO

The CMOs who participated in the SiriusDecisions study seem to have a view of CMO responsibilities that is aligned with our perspective. When talking to CMOs about approaching a role, or CEOs about hiring a CMO, we tell them that the fundamental elements a CMO must execute are to:

- Set goals
- Define (or refine) your strategy
- Build a plan that is designed to achieve those goals

- Execute the plan
- Optimize the plan when change inevitably happens
- Communicate results

Unfortunately, CMOs are not getting it done. Our assessment comes from over seventy collective years in marketing and business. Peter, for example, spent thirty years as a marketing practitioner, including a thirteen-year stint as an executive (five as the CMO) of a public software company that grew to $2 billion in annual revenue and made over a hundred acquisitions during his tenure. After leaving that company, he created our company to address these issues. Since then, we have reviewed well over a thousand marketing plans from companies of all sizes, industries, and levels of maturity.

Based on that large body of evidence, we can confidently posit that the issues are pervasive. We can also point to many instances in our own careers where we have struggled with each one of these core responsibilities. In other words, we are guilty too.

Assessing the Gaps

Let's explore some of the gaps in a little more detail. We have seen persistent issues in each of the following six areas:

1. **Inadequate (or** completely **absent) goals**
   Every marketing organization should have a clear set of objectives that are aligned to the overall business's objectives. The marketing objectives should have specific metrics, targets, and milestones defined. In practice, many marketing teams either don't have clear goals, or the goals aren't well communicated through the organization. In some cases, the goals are well defined, but there is no connection between the goals and the actual plan. Without a

direct connection between the goals and the plan, marketing goals start to feel like an aspirational suggestion.

2. **Poorly defined or communicated marketing strategy** The lack of a clear marketing strategy is one of the most significant causes of inefficiency in a marketing plan. Your marketing strategy is the means by which to make decisions about the appropriateness of marketing investment. For example, if you have a targeted account marketing strategy, a broad awareness approach might not be the best idea. You might instead leverage some Account-Based Marketing (ABM) tools to target your messages to the companies that are on your list. When we review a marketing plan and see a cornucopia of approaches, we often ask the marketing team to articulate their core marketing strategy. While the marketing leader can often describe their strategy clearly and specifically, the rest of the marketing team often struggles.

3. **A plan that is not designed to achieve your goals** The lack of goal alignment in marketing plans was one of our key motivations to write this book. When Peter reviewed marketing plans with marketing managers on his teams, he would ask how their activities were related to achieving the marketing goals. The typical response was a stunned silence, or at best, a loose connection to the overall goals. We find this is an issue with most teams.

4. **Ineffective execution**
   Here's some good news: if there is one thing that marketers are consistently good at doing, it is executing their plans. There are certainly cases where execution is a problem, but generally, marketers are really good at working toward a plan.

   The bigger issue is whether the plan is the *right* one, and designed to achieve your objectives.

5. **Failing to optimize the plan when change inevitably happens**
   Many marketers are good at optimizing tactics but few are good at optimizing the entire plan. If you look at digital marketing, you will find that most digital marketing managers are analytical and diligent when it comes to the optimization of their tactics. Marketing teams struggle with optimization when you start to think about optimizing across silos. For example, you might be optimizing your digital plan but neglecting the fact that you are struggling with sales tools further down the funnel. Or you may have a plan that includes a bunch of expensive events and under invests in digital campaigns. This level of optimization is most difficult because it involves moving resources and budgets between teams.

6. **Poor communication of results**
   It may seem counterintuitive given the vast amounts of data and visualization tools available to marketers, but they still struggle to communicate their results in a way that is meaningful to the business. One

problem that we often see is cherry-picking metrics or campaigns that look good versus showing the results of the total investment in marketing. We like to think about the concept of Return on Marketing Plan (RoMP), a view that considers your total investment across your entire plan and compares it to the aggregate result.

Another issue with telling an ROI story is the difficulty that people have calculating the full cost of a campaign. Most financial systems do not track cost by campaign, instead showing cost by department and general ledger (GL) code.

The most glaring issue with communicating marketing results is the inability to relate your investments and results to a set of aligned goals. When you communicate the results of your marketing investments to the executive committee or board, you need to be able to describe the results in the context of the business.

So, where is the love?

First of all, let's note that we appreciate marketers so much that our company requires us to spend all our time with them. One of the advantages of starting a company is picking your customers, and we think we have chosen wisely.

The marketers we have met over the past few decades are smart, creative, hard-working, and flexible people who are trying to do the right thing for their businesses.

The problem with marketing isn't the marketers—it's that the tools used to manage the marketing function have not caught up with the incredible change that the function has seen over the years. And while nearly every function in business has changed over time, the impact on marketing has been profound, making it harder than ever to be a marketing leader.

Some of the largest areas of change come from the digitization of marketing. Here are five.

1. **The Explosion of Data**
   The marketing function throws off a dizzying amount of data on a daily basis, often burying marketers in data without providing meaningful insights. At the same time, the expectations for those insights continue to increase. As a result, the majority of marketing data is thrown away because marketing teams don't have the skills or tools to handle all the details. Even the most sophisticated marketing teams, the ones with dedicated data scientists, can't handle the full complement of data created on a daily basis.

2. **Measuring What Can Be Measured**
   One major issue with all this marketing data is that it is not available equally across channels. While a typical Business to Business (B2B) marketer spends less than 20% of their budget on digital activities, their reporting is typically dominated by digital insights. All too often, we see management reports with deep analysis of the digital spend, and scant mention of the other 80% of their budget.

3. **Massive Increases in Complexity**
   The good news for marketers is that there are more choices than ever for spending their budget. The bad news is that there are more choices than ever. If you looked back at a marketing plan from twenty

years ago, you might see fifty line items in the plan. Today, it is easily in the hundreds, and sometimes in the thousands. While choice and granularity of the plan can be really helpful, it is increasingly difficult to manage a plan with that much complexity.

4. **Impatience in a Real-Time World**
   We have all been trained to expect immediate results. We can call a rideshare and expect a car to show up in three minutes, order something online and have it show up at our door within two days, and spin up a digital marketing initiative in about two minutes by clicking "promote this ad." That expectation of immediacy has made us less patient when it comes to getting results from marketing activities. An awareness campaign can take many months to move the needle as the results build. Content marketing efforts require consistent publishing, tweaking, and promotion over a long period of time to build a real audience.

5. **Difficulty Maintaining a Long-Term Strategic Perspective**
   Related to impatience, it is difficult for some executives to maintain a strategic perspective over a long period of time. But the best CMOs can think in minutes, days, weeks, quarters, years, and even decades. If you want to enter a new market, shift the competitive landscape, reposition a brand, or build enduring loyalty, you need to be able to define and execute initiatives that span quarters as well as fiscal planning periods.

Changing the Tools of the Trade

Despite all this change in the function of marketing, the tools marketers use have not changed in decades. Everyone's using the same slide decks and spreadsheets to manage marketing plans that were being used 25 years ago. Sure, things have evolved a little bit to leverage online versions, but essentially, they have not changed.

This may seem counterintuitive given the fact that there are over 7,000 marketing technology companies offering solutions in the market. But when you look at the data a little closer, you realize that the vast majority are focused on the delivery and optimization of one particular marketing channel versus the aggregate management of the marketing function.

A New Approach: A Framework for Operational Marketing Excellence

The majority of this book is dedicated to laying out a framework to help marketers improve their operational capabilities, and ultimately achieve operational excellence.

But first, we would like to explore the cost of inaction in the next chapter.

CHAPTER 2

The Impact of Ineffective Marketing Leadership Execution

We've established that marketing leaders face a lot of challenges that make it difficult to execute more effectively. But before you dismiss the challenges as too large, let's explore the significant financial and strategic cost of ignoring the underlying problems. In short, poor execution can not only be incredibly expensive, it can have long-lasting consequences for your business and your career.

Like many broad-reaching problems, the impact of ineffective marketing execution can be large and pervasive. We can break the impact into three major categories of ascending strategic importance: waste, sub-optimal performance, and poor strategic execution.

Category I: Waste

John Wanamaker, an early 20th century retail magnate, famously said, "Half the money I spend on advertising is wasted; the trouble is, I don't know which half."

More recently, Rakuten Advertising published a study in 2018[1] of 1000 marketing leaders who admitted that they waste about 26% of their budgets due to poor strategy or poor channel choices.

The glass-half-full analysis of those two quotes is that marketers have cut their waste by half in the last century. The glass-half-empty perspective would say that marketers are still losing more than one quarter of $1 trillion due to waste.

By analyzing thousands of budgets, we have identified the most common sources of waste in current marketing plans: unused budget, rush fees, non-strategic spending, duplicate spending, and over-paying.

Unused Budget

The primary responsibility of a marketing leader is to apply resources (both human and financial) toward initiatives that will help the organization achieve the most important marketing objectives. In other words, to spend money. Obviously, they should spend as little as possible for each individual service, media unit, or technology. However, they should spend as close to their full budget as possible – without going over – in order to achieve the best results for the money they planned to spend.

Surprisingly, this is a huge struggle for most marketing leaders. This comes from a lack of visibility into what has already been spent, and the inability to accurately forecast consumption of the remaining budget.

Because of the lack of visibility, many marketers conservatively forecast their spending to avoid going over. As a result, we consistently see that marketers leave a lot of their budget unspent.

The top-performing cohort of budget owners that we have analyzed leave somewhere between 5% to 10% of their budget

---

[1] Rakuten Advertising Press Release "Marketers admit 26% of their budget will be wasted in 2018", March 2018

unspent. More typically, we see somewhere between 10% and 20% of budgets left unspent. And in some extreme cases, we see people leaving more than a third of their budget on the table.

Think of it this way: If you are managing a $10 million budget, wouldn't you benefit from an incremental $1 million to spend?

Rush Fees

Marketing spending is rarely done in a straight line. The typical behavior that we see is slow spending at the beginning of a fiscal quarter, rapidly accelerating in the last few weeks of the quarter. A best practice is to spread your spending more evenly through the fiscal period.

This panic buying phenomenon is exacerbated in environments that have a "use it or lose it" policy in place. Marketers often look for ways to consume their budget as it becomes clear that they're not spending enough toward the end of their quarter.

When the timeline to spend money is short, we often see marketers pay a premium to get things done quickly. Agencies and service providers often charge rush fees to complete their projects in time to account for the cost by the end of the quarter.

Non-Strategic Spending

There are two primary drivers of non-strategic spending. The first is related to the last-minute spending that some marketers carry out just to consume their budget. We hear stories all the time of people who justify spending a lot of money on t-shirts or other promotional items because they were going to lose the budget anyway.

The other driver of nonstrategic spending comes from the inability of most financial systems to organize and track spending by campaign rather than by financial categories, like GL codes. Ideally, you should spend the vast majority of your budget on campaigns that are producing the results you need to achieve your goals. Without the ability to track campaign-related spending, marketers fall into the trap of spending on a non-strategic list of stuff. We like to call this "random acts of marketing."

Duplicate Spending

Have you ever designed the same campaign or creative asset more than once? It happens far more often than you might expect. As marketing teams get larger and more complex, the risk of duplicate spending increases significantly.

There are two ways to think about duplicate spending. The first one is when an organization literally does the same thing twice. The second, and far more common, is when an organization spends money on creating something new instead of fully leveraging assets that have been developed elsewhere in the organization.

This phenomenon occurs in almost every large organization with 100+ marketers and happens with surprising frequency in much smaller organizations. Why? Because teams don't have clear visibility into what's happening in every part of the organization.

Over-Paying

A frequent conversation topic among CMOs is the appropriate amount to spend for a particular product or service. How much should you pay for a PR agency? How much did you pay for that marketing technology? How much did you pay for SEO services?

Our data tells us that some people are significantly overpaying for certain products and services.

Determining the appropriate amount to pay for a product or service is typically achieved through either direct experience or tapping into your personal network. Ideally, marketers would have a set of benchmarks to determine how much their peers have paid for similar services. Without these types of benchmarks, almost everyone will overpay for some of the line items in their marketing plan.

Category II: Sub-Optimal Performance

While directly wasted budget is the easiest impact to understand, you may see an even larger negative consequence if your team fails to deliver the results contemplated in the plan. This can happen when you don't hit your targets, set the wrong targets, fail to tune and balance, or spend more than your budget.

Not Hitting Your Targets

If you don't put all your budget to work in a timely manner, focused on the most important initiatives, you have a higher likelihood of missing your targets. Missing your targets has a multilayered impact on your marketing organization. First, if your targets are directly related to achieving financial results, you quickly enter a negative spiral of ever-smaller budgets. Secondly, you also erode the credibility of the marketing team.

Setting the Wrong Targets

Sometimes the problem with performance achievement versus target is more related to the original targets than to the performance. Like a sales leader setting a sales plan, one of the most important skills of a marketing leader is setting, defending, and implementing the right targets that define the success of the organization.

A target that is set too high can have obvious consequences. Along with a high likelihood of missing the target, artificially high targets erode the morale of a marketing organization, because the team doesn't believe the plan is achievable from day one.

Targets that are set too low also have consequences. Some organizations then become complacent, only to get a strong dose of reality when someone decides to benchmark the performance of their team.

Marketing teams that are too complacent sometimes "take their foot off the gas" when they achieve their objectives, which ultimately limits their potential achievement, opening the door for competitive threats. Great marketing leaders are consistently able to strike the right balance between setting challenging and achievable targets.

Lack of Tuning and Balancing

A plan that is not continually measured, tuned, and balanced, can erode over time. One phenomenon that we often see is an over-reliance on physical events. In some sectors, physical events are quite popular because of the high visibility, familiarity, and built-in inertia. But, physical events tend to require long-term planning with some financial commitment made well in advance. That long lead time makes it much more difficult to make adjustments to plans that have a significant amount of event spending.

Beyond the tuning and balancing based on mix, almost any marketing effort can be improved over time through constant tuning of message, audience, creative, or other approaches. Unless this discipline is deeply ingrained in your approach, you will not reach the full potential return for your marketing investment.

Additionally, a well-balanced marketing plan addresses all phases of the customer lifecycle from awareness, to consideration, to conversion, through repeat purchase and referral.

Spending More Than Your Budget

We discussed the challenge related to spending less than your allocated budget. Spending more than your budget can result in an outsized negative impact.

Depending on the size of the overage, the impact can go beyond marketing performance and create a problem with overall company profitability. There have been a few famous instances of runaway spending on campaigns that caused companies to miss their quarterly earnings projections, but it is far more common for marketing teams to bruise their reputations for good fiscal management.

Category III: Poor Strategic Execution

The most severe long-term pain is felt when marketing teams are unable to execute their strategic agenda. In some cases, poor strategic execution can be hard to measure. You get the feeling that the company is just not living up to its potential. The tip of the spear when it comes to company execution is often the marketing team. They're charged with defining target markets, codifying the vision, providing visibility, building pipeline, communicating with the market, and much, much more. When the marketing team is unable to execute their agenda to its fullest extent, the company will not realize its potential. When companies don't operate at peak performance, they are at risk of being beaten by the competition—companies that execute more effectively. Losing your position in a market often happens in slow motion, but companies struggle to change their go-to-market strategy because they "have always done it that way."

The Ultimate Accountability

What is the ultimate cost of not effectively executing your marketing agenda? If you are a senior marketing leader, then it's your job. In the worst case, it's your career.

So, what's the good news? There are some straightforward actions you can take that will make a huge difference in your ability to execute. The remaining chapters provide a practical roadmap to improving your operational capabilities, delivering more value for your organization, and accelerating your own career.

CHAPTER 3

The Elements of Operational Marketing Excellence

If the impact of ineffective marketing leadership execution is so high, why don't more people try to solve the problem? In most cases, the issue is not a lack of effort, but the lack of all of the core elements required for operational excellence.

When these elements are combined, a marketing organization can get much closer to its true potential. A single missing component can throw everything in the entire system off. The marketing leader in an organization needs to operate like the conductor of an orchestra, the NASA mission commander, or even a classroom teacher in charge of wrangling a bunch of adolescents. These organizations and systems all require the following five elements:

1. **A strategy-driven and goals-based planning approach**
   Whether your objectives are to put an astronaut on the surface of the moon or to help a group of kids achieve their academic goals, you need to clearly define success with measurable goals, metrics, targets, and milestones. You also need to define a

strategy for achieving success and break it down into manageable chunks, or "campaigns" in marketing parlance.

2. **A complete system view**
   The more complex the system, the more important it is to develop a broad view of it. The conductor of the orchestra doesn't just focus on the performance, she also considers the practice regimens, the development of future talent, fundraising, promotion, the temperature in the theatre, and the changing tastes in music for the community.

3. **A process for measurement, refinement and optimization**
   A lucky leader can achieve their objectives once, but it takes an ongoing focus on measurement, optimization, and improvement to achieve ongoing success.

4. **The discipline to connect all activities to outcomes**
   Achieving operational excellence means doing all the right things and not wasting time on the wrong things. Many organizations get stuck in the rut of doing the same things that they have always done, over and over. To deliver results with efficiency, you need to continue to ask the question "To what end?" when you are evaluating your activities. By understanding the relationship of outcomes to activities, an efficient leader can develop the right mix that will achieve the best results within the available resources.

5. **A culture of excellence**

Since an organization's achievement is a team sport, it is impossible to deliver consistently excellent results without everyone delivering. A key responsibility of a leader is to define and demonstrate the expectations of the organization. In this way, a great leader can significantly improve organizational effectiveness.

Next, let's explore the specific application of these five elements within the context of a marketing organization.

I. A strategy-based and goal-driven planning approach

For most of us, defining and aligning the extended team on your goals is the first step in the planning process. There are some instances where there are prerequisites to this step. For example, if you are starting a business or going through a significant change, you would start by understanding and documenting the market, customers, messages, etc.

Defining a core set of goals, metrics, targets, and milestones

In order to describe your plan at the right level of detail, we recommend that you define four to six objectives for the marketing organization. You need enough goals to comprehensively define what success means, and enough detail in each of the goals so there is absolutely no doubt about the achievement. A properly defined goal includes a descriptive title, metrics, targets and milestones:

A descriptive title: The title of the goal should provide a clear definition of success itself, for instance: "Create $10 million of marketing generated pipeline in 2020," or "Enter the French market and close at least one customer by the end of Q2."

Metrics: The metrics are the tools that you will use to measure success. For example: marketing-generated pipeline, sales qualified leads (SQLs), new logo acquisition, and annual recurring revenue (ARR).

Targets: Metrics alone don't tell you much. You also need to define what measurement you will achieve. For example, if the metric is marketing generated pipeline, the target could be $25 million.

Milestones: In some cases, you need to define milestones to make sure that you are on track to achieve your targets. Using the example above of $25 million in pipeline, you could define quarterly objectives of $4 million, $8 million, $15 million, and $25 million to reflect the growth and seasonality that you would expect along the way.

Getting aligned with your strategy

The term "strategy" is one of the most overused and misunderstood terms in business. That's a bad combination.

In its simplest form, a strategy is the approach that you choose to attempt to achieve your objectives. For example, if your goal is to climb a mountain, you can choose a meandering trail that is longer, but has a shallower incline, or you can choose to scramble up the steep, sheer face. Both paths will lead to the same goal, but they might involve different tactics and equipment. The sheer face could require ropes and other safety equipment, while the meandering trail might require food, more water, and even sleeping gear if it takes you longer than a single day to achieve your objective. To plan your hike, you need to choose your strategy in advance. And if you are hiking with a group, all of the members need to be aligned on your strategy.

A marketing strategy follows the same rules. If your primary objective is adding $25 million of new pipeline, there are many strategies you can choose to achieve the goal. And while you can define strategies at all levels (for example a campaign strategy, or even a strategy for a landing page), you need to align your team with your overall marketing strategy.

Successful marketing organizations have a well-aligned top-level marketing strategy. HubSpot, the CRM software company, is a great example of a company that was built on a strategy that they coined as "inbound marketing"—or what would be generically called thought leadership and content marketing. Professional services like law or accounting firms often use a combination of branding and client hospitality. By inviting their clients to sponsored events, activities, and conferences, they can create opportunities for their partners to have one-on-one conversations with prospective clients.

If you sell a low-cost consumer product, you might be successful by using the HubSpot strategy, but the relatively low-value customer relationships would not justify the client hospitality approach used by a large public accounting firm.

Choosing your strategy and aligning your team on it is incredibly important. To go back to the mountain climbing example, if you choose to take the long meandering trail without aligning with everyone, you may have team members who don't have enough water or a sleeping bag.

Defining the constraints for your plan

Because we all operate in the real world, we have to plan for existing conditions. For example, you probably have profitability goals for your business that will define your budget envelope. You may have existing commitments as you enter the new year including retainers, contracted events, software contracts, and lease agreements.

Along with these commitments, you need to understand your organizational capabilities. If you want to move from a digital demand model to a thought leadership model, you may need to hire new people, or plan for some additional contract resources.

Build thematic campaigns aligned with the metrics in the goals

Armed with a set of goals, aligned on a strategy, and with your constraints in the plan, the next step is to build a set of thematic campaigns that are designed to achieve your objectives.

The term "campaign" is also overused in marketing these days, which can make it difficult to build campaigns at the right level. One good test is to see if you can align the metrics for your campaign with the metrics for your goals. If your goal in question is to grow pipeline, the metric is pipeline created. If your "campaign" is designed to generate leads, clicks, views, or registrations, then it probably isn't a campaign. In this case, it is a tactic that could be part of a broader campaign. If you bundle together the lead generation tactics with a nurturing effort, the combined effort can be measured in pipeline contribution.

If your campaigns are aligned with your goal metrics, you can easily build a capacity plan to achieve your objectives. Each campaign should also have a campaign manager who is accountable for delivering on the results.

A campaign plan designed to achieve your pipeline objectives might look like this:

Pipeline Campaign	Budget	Q1 Milestone	Q2 Milestone	Q3 Milestone	Q4 Milestone
US ABM	$2M	$2M	$4M	$8M	$12M
WW Digital	$1.5M	$2M	$3M	$6M	$10M
EMEA ABM	$1M	$1M	$2M	$3M	$6M
TOTAL	**$4.5M**	**$5M**	**$9M**	**$17M**	**$28M**
Pipeline Goal		$4M	$8M	$15M	$25M
Coverage		125%	113%	113%	112%

In the case above, the campaign plan is built to deliver 112% of the target for pipeline throughout the year. Each campaign has a budget and should also have a campaign manager who is accountable for delivering on both the budget target and the results.

Each campaign may contain many underlying tactics that are required to achieve the results. The campaign manager is responsible for making sure that the tactics are delivering the interim results required for their target overall, but they are ultimately responsible for delivering against a common set of objectives that can be normalized across the plan.

II. A complete marketing system view

Building a comprehensive campaign plan to achieve your objectives is a necessary (and critical) element of marketing leadership. Operationally excellent leaders also develop and monitor a complete system-wide view of marketing for their company.

As you are executing your plan, it is critical that you regularly review the health of the overall marketing system to make sure that everything is operating efficiently. If you think of your progress toward your objectives as the GPS in your car, the complete system view is similar to the check engine lights, dashboard alerts, and tune-up computer at your service station.

For example, if you are focused on pipeline development for your plan objectives, you may miss the fact that you are not nurturing leads that could convert to opportunities, or you may not be taking advantage of upsell and cross-sell opportunities.

To support these analytics, we developed a diagnostic tool called The Integrated Marketing Machine (Figure 1). The tool is meant to highlight all the interconnected parts of a go-to-market system. While most marketers do a good job measuring their lead to opportunity funnel, other parts of the system are often ignored.

Marketing system metrics versus goal metrics

The metrics associated with your marketing system are usually different from the metrics for achieving your goals. Like the diagnostics in your car, the marketing system is typically instrumented to warn when a system is operating outside an expected range. Pipeline conversion metrics are a good example of this type of measurement. Your marketing qualified to sales qualified lead conversion may have an expected conversion rate of 60% - 80%. If your conversion rate is lower than 60%, marketing is probably passing too many unqualified leads. If the conversion rate is higher than 80%, marketing may have a filter that is too tight.

Presence tests

Another application of the marketing system view is to make sure that all the appropriate systems are in place. For example, do you have a process to nurture leads that fall out of each stage of the funnel? Do you have a program to market new solutions to your existing customers for cross-sell or upsell? Have you explored all the potential demand sources that could create opportunities in your pipeline?

By regularly reviewing this complete system view, you force yourself to ask questions about the effectiveness of each element of your marketing system, and to make sure all the elements are represented in your plan.

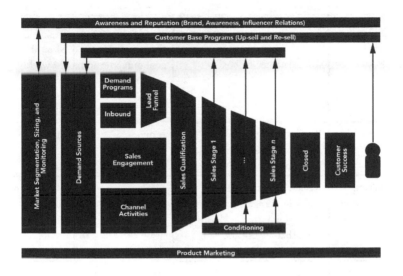

Figure 1: The Integrated Marketing Machine

III. A process for measurement, refinement and optimization

There are two primary issues we often see with metrics and dashboards: either they lack context and don't have any targets and milestones, or nobody looks at them at all. A key to operational success is a process and regular set of reviews that focus on the "So what?" that comes from the data.

To facilitate review of relevant data, we recommend that you schedule a series of focused meetings with the appropriate stakeholders to review the data in question. When reviewing metrics, the data should be presented with a comparison to their targets, milestones, and operating ranges (where appropriate).

Meeting	Purpose	Stakeholders	Frequency
Goal progress reviews	Monitor the progress toward achieving goals	Owner of the goal outcome and any underlying campaign owners	Monthly (bi-weekly for higher velocity businesses)
Plan review	Review the aggregate performance against all the goals	Individual goal owners	Monthly
Marketing system review	Review the presence and operating range for all marketing systems. Highlight areas that are outside expected performance	Marketing leadership	Monthly (or quarterly)
Market scan	Review any changes to the external market conditions, competition, or major industry shifts	Marketing and product management	Quarterly or when a major market event happens
Budget review and refinement	Review committed spend, budget burn rate (BBR), forecast of spend vs. plan, and plan accruals	Marketing budget owners and finance team	Monthly (or bi-weekly for higher velocity businesses)
Campaign reviews	Review campaign performance vs. expectations for campaigns in flight, determine whether to repeat or refine	Marketing leadership, campaign owners	Monthly or on completion of major campaign
Quarterly business reviews	Report on progress vs. expected results for entire plan, marketing system review status, and campaign performance review summary	Marketing and business leadership	Quarterly
Strategy review	Assess marketing strategy effectiveness and make recommendations for adjustments	Marketing and business leadership	Semiannually

This may seem like a lot of meetings, but they are important elements of an operationally excellent marketing process. And if you are part of a small team, you can incorporate several of these reviews into the same meeting. Many marketing teams meet regularly for generic status meetings. If that is the case, you can turn your meetings into a much more productive investment of your time with a purposeful agenda.

IV. The discipline to connect all activities to outcomes

If you don't have a constant focus on understanding the relationship between your activities and meaningful outcomes for your business, you can quickly devolve into what we call "random acts of marketing." And while it is a fool's errand to connect a financial value to every marketing activity, you must connect every marketing activity to a financial outcome. In other words, you don't need to try to attribute $2.73 to each data sheet you produce, but you do need to understand that the purpose of the sales tool is to increase the conversion rate of a certain stage in the sales cycle.

To what end?

One effective technique for assessing the value of your activities is to ask the question "To what end?" until you can connect the activity to a line on the Profit and Loss statement (P&L). For example, let's take that data sheet you are writing:

We want to create a data sheet.

To what end? To help the sales team convert stage 1 opportunities into stage 2 opportunities.

To what end? To get more opportunities through the funnel and close new revenue.

Now let's take a look at something harder to measure, like a customer appreciation award:

> We want to offer a customer appreciation award.
>
> **To what end?** To create more loyalty with that customer.
>
> **To what end?** To get them to renew their contract AND get them to act as a reference.
>
> **To what end?** To close new revenue, reduce churn, and acquire new customers.

Even if you can't distill each activity down to a numerical value, it is important to understand the business (financial) motivation for the activity. If you can't make that connection, maybe you should stop the activity.

Alignment to goals

Another approach is to connect your activities to your overall goals. If you have done a complete job of defining your marketing objectives, you should be able to associate the vast majority of your underlying activities with one of those objectives.

If you find a common set of activities that cannot be associated with any of your goals, you might consider adding another goal since its importance is implied by your activities. If you can't define - or justify - that additional goal, it's time to stop the random acts of marketing.

V. A culture of excellence

The best operational leaders can fail if they don't have the full support of their team behind them. Additionally, the operational rigor of an organization can be quickly eroded if you accept deviance from your cultural values. The secret to getting your entire team behind you is to build a culture of operational excellence. Culture comes from the top, so it is critical that marketing leadership embraces the following principles:

Focus on truth, not credit

The best marketing teams operate like scientists, not promoters. You can tell which type of group you have when it comes to quarterly review time. The promoters focus on all the good parts of the last quarter and gloss over (or worse, hide) any negative results. The scientists are always seeking truth, even if the truth isn't very attractive. When promoters report on their results, they often cherry pick only the good campaigns or channels. The scientists will report out on all the channels and campaigns, highlighting the outlying performers - both positive and negative. When reporting on negative results, the scientists will develop a theory for the poor performance, and may even design an experiment to try to prove that theory with upcoming campaigns.

One key indicator of a culture of marketing promoters is the amount of "marketing influence" in their results. Marketing influence can be an important metric, especially with long, complex sales cycles. But when all positive news is in the form of marketing influence, it is time to find some scientists.

Celebrate success and learning

A guaranteed way to discourage marketers from reporting the truth is to punish them for reporting negative results. Don't confuse negative results with mistakes. In some cases, poor performance is due to a mistake, and there should be accountability in your organization. But poor performance may come from an assumption that was proven wrong. That's how you learn.

So how do you avoid the "everyone gets a trophy" mentality? You reward and celebrate success *and* you celebrate insights from experiments that can turn into future performance improvement. If a marketer presents results that didn't perform as expected and then shrugs when you ask why the campaign didn't perform well, they don't deserve any praise. But if a marketer can articulate the assumption they made, the data that proves the assumption was wrong, the impact of that assumption, and how they will improve future campaigns, they definitely deserve your praise.

Embrace diversity

Diverse organizations perform better because they see the same problems with different lenses. The best marketing organizations are excellent at identifying changes in the market, their campaign performance, their competition, etc. By identifying and responding to change rapidly, marketing teams can outpace their peers and deliver much higher performance.

One of the best ways to identify change is to look at problems from different perspectives. If your entire team is cut from the same cloth, you can quickly convince yourself that your perspective is the only one that matters.

Develop emerging talent

One way to make sure that you have fresh perspectives in your organization is to embrace the idea that the development of emerging talent is a critical, ongoing process. One of the best ways to reward up-and-coming talent is to give them a special project to work on. It costs nothing, and you often end up with excellent results.

Furthermore, there are lots of reasons for opportunities to emerge in your organization, including turnover (voluntary and involuntary), growth, or positions that become available when other high performers in your organization take on a new assignment. The best operational leaders will always have someone ready to fill those unexpected vacancies - temporarily or permanently - with emerging talent from your team.

CHAPTER 4

Your Marketing DNA: Stakeholders and Culture

Great plans are only successful when they're executed by great teams. In this chapter, we focus on how to assemble the team that maximizes your chances of repeatable success.

In order to deliver a successful plan, you must identify and organize all your marketing stakeholders. If you operate in a large company, you may have multiple team members in many of the key stakeholder roles. If you work in a small company, you may find that one or two individuals wear most of the stakeholder hats between them.

You will also likely find that some of the stakeholder roles are filled by people who aren't full-time employees (FTE), but are instead contractors, consultants or agencies. How the stakeholder roles are filled is less important for the purposes of this topic than understanding what the roles are, and ensuring that the responsibilities are understood and owned by someone on your team.

The 7 stakeholders of a marketing plan and budget

CMO: The CMO (or VP of Marketing, if that's how your company is structured) is the executive leader and owner of the marketing plan and budget. The CMO is accountable for committing the marketing organization to achieving a certain set of valuable outcomes given a budget that they negotiate with the company. Once he or she has buy-in and support from the CEO and executive peers, the CMO must clearly communicate the goals, metrics of success, and high-level strategies to the broader marketing organization. He or she must ensure team alignment and delegate responsibility for spending budget, executing campaigns, and reporting on results throughout the team.

Marketing Director: One or more marketing directors typically report to the CMO. They are often responsible for a marketing function such as public relations, demand generation, or product marketing. Depending on the company structure, the marketing director might be responsible for a region. Given their seniority and the nature of their role, marketing directors typically are given responsibility for a portion of the budget, and then it's up to them to figure out how to spend that across campaigns and other activities in order to achieve the marketing goals they've understood from the CMO. The marketing director must ensure that his or her team members have a clear understanding of goals, target metrics, time frames, and strategy.

The marketing plan and budget stakeholder chart

Campaign Manager: Campaign managers are accountable for designing, coordinating and executing the campaigns that will achieve the marketing goals. They are often functional specialists. For example, there may be a digital demand campaign manager, or someone dedicated to running the company's events. They frequently receive a target budget from one or more of the marketing directors, which defines the spending envelope for their particular campaign. Campaign managers must be operationally strong, have excellent project management and coordination skills, and possess superior communication capabilities. The role of campaign manager has declined in the last fifteen years or so with the rise of channel-oriented focus. There is a dedicated section at the end of this chapter, making the case for the reemergence of the campaign manager role.

Marketing Individual Contributors: "Marketing ICs" are typically responsible for the majority of the actual spending in a marketing budget. They will source and purchase the items and services necessary for running the campaign. As such, they need to possess both marketing and financial acumen. They need to be detail-oriented and rigorous in updating their activities and data to ensure that campaigns are executed well and on time, and to ensure there is always current and accurate metric and expense data on hand to generate meaningful reports.

Marketing Operations: "Marketing Ops" is the fastest growing role in marketing organizations. It is a multi-disciplinary role that encompasses finance, technology, analytics, operations and marketing skills. Marketing operations influences plan and budget set up. They enable the team to be successful by implementing and monitoring the tools, systems and data they need to execute effectively. They also capture, synthesize and report on the progress of the marketing plan and budget, including forecasts and recommended course corrections.

Sales: Sales is a critical stakeholder for almost every marketing organization. Since marketing is largely occupied with generating awareness and interest in a company's offerings in order for sales to close deals on them, it is of paramount importance that sales and marketing are well-aligned at the beginning of the planning and budgeting cycle. Sales needs to understand what it can and can't expect from marketing. The sales leader must ensure there are sufficient sales resources to handle the pipeline generated by marketing, and marketing needs to be sure that it is neither over- nor under-feeding the sales team with well-qualified leads. As the year progresses, sales represents one of the most important voices in terms of gauging progress and identifying course corrections needed in the marketing plan.

Finance: No other function spends like marketing. Everyone in marketing spends, and they spend quickly on hugely diverse items from incidental expenses to major investments. A strong relationship between finance and marketing will make everyone's life easier in the company. Marketing needs to make friends with finance, align processes, understand mutual accountabilities, and work together to ensure marketing budget and expense data is kept as current and accurate as possible. Fresh financial data means that marketers can make confident, well-informed purchasing decisions at the rate they need to in order to achieve their marketing goals on time. Inefficient finance-marketing relationships create budget, execution and business risk.

A note on Information Technology (IT): There is an argument that IT should be one of the key stakeholders in the delivery of a successful marketing plan and budget, and you will not witness strong pushback on that idea here. Indeed, as marketing technology (MarTech) continues to grow in scale and diversity, the partnership between marketing and IT is critical. We have chosen not to include IT in this view for two reasons. The first is an effort to keep the model succinct. The second is that a strong marketing operations leader can, and should, act as an effective liaison between marketing and IT. If you think it makes sense to include IT as a key stakeholder in your plan and budget, you should go for it.

Creating Accountability for Stakeholders with the IOU Model

It's critically important that the marketing stakeholders understand the IOU model, which is a simplified version of a RACI (Responsible, Accountable, Consulted, Informed) model.

I stands for **influence**. An influencer is not ultimately responsible for a task, but should be involved in defining and shaping the task.

O stands for **own**. If a stakeholder owns a task, the buck stops there. Owners are ultimately responsible for the definition and outcome of a task.

U stands for **understand**. If stakeholders are required to understand a task, they may not be involved in its creation or definition, but they are accountable for understanding how the task affects them, and what they need to do to contribute towards it.

The Marketing IOU chart maps accountability levels for the key tasks involved in creating and running a successful marketing plan and budget:

If you are able to identify the stakeholders and the IOU model for your marketing organization, you will have a significantly greater chance of success in delivering your marketing plan. You will achieve greater clarity throughout your organization, higher efficiency, and more accurate communication and data sharing. Your stakeholder and IOU model might look slightly different from the examples shared in this chapter, but if you apply this framework in a way that makes sense for your organization, you will benefit throughout the year.

	CMO	Marketing Director	Campaign Manager	Marketing IC	Marketing Ops	Sales	Finance
Secure overall budget	O	U	U	U	U	U	I
Define topline objectives	O	U	U	U	U	I	I
Set qualitative goals	O	U	U	U	U	I	U
Define metrics of achievement	O	I	U	U	U	U	U
Obtain alignment and buy-in	O	I	U	U	U	U	U
Communicate results	O	I	U	U	U	U	U
Course-correct through the year	O	I	U	U	U	U	U
Set team goals	O	I	U	U	U		
Allocate budget across team	O	I			U		
Define marketing strategies to achieve goals	I	O	U	U	U		
Select campaigns to achieve strategies	I	O	I	U	U		
Manage subset of budget	U	O	U	U	I		
Interlock expenses with accounting	U	O	U	U	I		I
Execute campaigns	U	I	O	I	U		
Manage expenses day-to-day	U	I	I	O	I		I
Report on progress and results	I	U	U	U	O	U	U
Analyze ROI of activities	I	U	U	U	O	U	U
Reconcile expenses	U	U	U	I	O		I

Key
O = Owns
I = Influences
U = Understands
N/A

The marketing plan and budget IOU chart

Assessing Your Marketing DNA

There are several dimensions of a business' structure that influence which parts of the marketing mix you should invest most heavily in, which you should manage and execute with in-house vs. outsourced staff, and so on. When considering your marketing organization in total, it's important to run through these elements and to ensure that your team structure and culture are well-aligned with the type of business in which you operate.

If your marketing team DNA isn't a match for your company DNA, it will be more difficult for you to set effective goals, and to execute them efficiently. Below are 4 categories of DNA traits to consider as you design and hone the marketing structure you need to best support your organization.

1. Centralized, internal agency, matrixed, or integrated

It is critically important to have clear alignment between the marketing organizational structure and the corresponding corporate structure.

Small and medium businesses frequently have a single, *centralized* marketing organization. The CMO reports into the CEO and sits on the executive team, and manages a unified marketing organization that serves the company functionally.

As companies grow, they may establish strategic business units that operate as mini companies within the broader organization. Their leaders normally have a high degree of profit and Loss (P&L) responsibility and strategic autonomy. It is critically important to gain alignment on how marketing will serve such a structure. It might operate as an **internal agency**, utilized by all the business units, with the business units operating as customers who each contribute a portion of the marketing budget.

In a **matrixed** model, some marketing functions might be absorbed into the business units, with other functions served by the CMO organization. For example, product marketing, field marketing, and even demand generation might move into the strategic business unit, with other functions (e.g. PR, branding, events) remaining at the corporate level.

Finally, marketing might be more completely separated and **integrated** into the business units. If this happens, it might require the establishment of a separate corporate marketing team that manages the corporate brand, corporate events, etc., with a very high degree of autonomy granted to the strategic business units (SBU's) for their own day-to-day marketing needs.

Whatever structure you operate within, the entire marketing organization should be clear on their responsibilities to each other and to the business. They should be prepared for frequent change, too. As the company structure evolves, the marketing team structure is likely to evolve along with it.

2. Service, solution, technology, product, or platform

Often overlooked, it is imperative to have organizational clarity about what it is you are marketing. Consider the five-way split below. As you can see, the characteristics of different offer types have different features that drive different types of marketing requirements. These features should influence the structure of your marketing plan and strategy, and therefore your team:

Feature	Service	Solution	Technology	Product	Platform
Degree of Customization	●	◕	◕	○	○
Resistance to disruption	○	◕	●	◕	◕
Technical differentiation	◕	◕	●	◕	◕
Vertical specialization needed	●	●	○	●	◕
Solves one complete business problem	◕	◕	◕	●	●
Solves >1 complete business problems	◕	○	◕	○	●
Speed of time-to-market	○	◕	○	●	●
Tangible assets delivered	○	◕	●	●	●
Repeatability	○	◕	●	●	●
Gross margin	◕	◕	●	●	●
Revenue driven by	Labor	License + Labor	License	License	License
	Very Low	*Low*	*Medium*	*High*	*Very High*
Key	○	◕	◑	◔	●

Marketing considerations for different types of offering

3. B2C or B2B

This distinction is primarily occupied with the different marketing mix compositions of business-to-consumer (B2C) and business-to-business (B2B) companies. Based on those mixes, it's likely that marketing leaders will emphasize hiring in-house versus outsourced talent pools differently. This is a complex topic that could warrant its own book, so what follows is a high-level overview. You should assess the skill sets you most want to maintain with full-time employees and what is outsourced to consultants and contractors.

B2C marketing is *typically* focused on broad communication vehicles that can appeal to buyers' emotions like advertising and awareness campaigns on digital, TV and radio. In B2C, marketers normally operate with a lower customer acquisition cost (CAC), on average. For high-priced items like cars or university courses, the CAC may still run high, but the channels of mass marketing or mass customization (versus highly-personalized marketing) is the norm. Because B2C marketing tends to be heavily digital, it is common to find smaller teams with a higher spend per team-member, as well as a higher use of brand and advertising agencies. Metrics tend to be focused on impressions, clicks, brand perceptions, digital analytics and data visualization.

B2B typically has longer sales cycles than B2C. It is more complex, less emotion-driven, the buying processes have more rounds of approval, security, procurement, finance, competitive bids, etc. It is characterized by team buying rather than individual buying. B2B marketing, therefore, tends to pick its prospects very carefully and invest more in targeting them based on their profile, persona and buyer characteristics. Once identified, B2B marketing will provide customized - even personalized - content to capture and retain the attention of prospects through the buying cycle.

B2B marketing tends to have larger in-house teams and greater investment in product marketing, events teams, in-house PR teams, field marketing, sales enablement case-studies, thought leadership—and likely, marketing operations.

Some product-led-growth (PLG) software as a service (SaaS) companies have more heavily adopted B2C marketing strategies even though they are clearly selling a B2B product. It is worth understanding whether your company falls into this category, ensuring that there is alignment around the key activities you will need to carry out to best serve your go-to-market motion, and structuring accordingly.

4. International or domestic

When a business becomes international, marketing complexity significantly grows. Strategically, you need to create your marketing plan according to your market presence, brand awareness, perception, and competitive strength across multiple regions with disparate requirements.

You must take into account cultural, economic, and regulatory differences across multiple countries. For example, there is a substantial difference in security and privacy regulations around the globe. This will materially impact how, and to whom, you may advertise.

You will need to understand how your budget should be managed, bearing in mind that you will be generating expenses in more than one currency, and that these will ultimately all need to be managed within a budget of a single currency.

As the company grows, the marketing organization needs to grow internationally with it, and it needs to be structured to address international needs in the context of all the other DNA attributes.

Putting it into practice

The Marketing DNA review described in this chapter highlights a number of sometimes complex questions to consider as you structure your team and culture over time. It's not something so simple that it can be captured in a scorecard, but it does need to be considered thoughtfully, and revisited regularly, to ensure that you are continuously evolving your organization to stay in lockstep with the needs of the business.

As your company evolves, you will need to change the structure, organization and management of your marketing team. This is one of the reasons why the culture of the company, and of your marketing team, is so worthy of your continuous focus and attention. Flexible teams with great communication and high degrees of trust will be better suited to the inevitable change that successful companies require of them. We recommend integrating a DNA review, and operational adjustment, into your strategic planning process. This will help you ensure your marketing operation is always aligned with your strategy.

Bring back campaign management

Earlier in this chapter, we mentioned the importance of the campaign manager, and the fact that the role is far less prevalent than it once was. We believe marketing would be better off with the re-emergence of the marketing campaign management role.

If you run a search for "what does a campaign manager do?" most of the results are about political campaign managers. In many respects, a presidential campaign is the ultimate marketing campaign, but you really need to dig for other real-world examples of marketing campaign management. Let's look at the political campaign, and see how closely it mirrors a marketing campaign. Both make an offer, have a clear goal, and a clear metric. In politics, the offer is the candidate, the goal is to win the election, and the metric is the number of votes. In marketing, the offer is a product or service, the goal is to get people to buy the product or service, and the metric is the number of sales.

In both cases, the campaign has a budget that can be spent in an endlessly diverse set of ways. The core campaign messages are intended to elicit a specific response, and are delivered via an integrated, multichannel marketing campaign that employs TV, print, digital, in-person events, billboards, social, radio, etc. The team continuously measures performance and optimizes to tune and refine the channels, the message, and the audience segmentation. In politics, a campaign manager is responsible for orchestrating the entire campaign to promote the offer—the candidate. A good offer with a bad campaign won't succeed, and vice versa.

The campaign manager is personally responsible for three key things:

1. Validating the offer's appeal
2. Defining the message
3. Targeting the right audience

Without these three things, the campaign will inevitably perform suboptimally with disparate messages over the wrong channels to the wrong audiences. The campaign will be disjointed, and overall campaign performance will be impossible to measure. If no one owns the message, audience, and offer, how can you tell whether things are going well?

Given the strategic impact of the political campaign manager role, where are all the campaign managers in marketing?

If you search job sites for campaign manager vacancies, you'll notice that the job descriptions are not strategic leadership roles at all. Rather, they tend to be project management roles with a preference for some digital marketing skills. These are critical skills for many marketing campaigns, to be sure, but they do not describe the entirety of the marketing campaign management role. Campaign managers used to exist in marketing teams, but the emergence of channel-dedicated technologies and tools has led to a channel-first mindset in marketing structure and measurement. The campaign manager role has been sidelined, but we believe it's time for marketing campaign management to make a comeback.

Marketing Campaign Management is to CMOs what Product Management Is to CEOs

Good product managers are hard to find, but the very best among them treat their product lines like their business. Of course, they have constraints, but the best product managers take ownership of every aspect of the product life cycle: strategy, roadmap, technical decisions, pricing, value prop, target market, competitive dynamics, sales enablement, profitability, growth, engineering management—everything. Do they own all of those things on the org chart? No, probably not. But they feel accountable and act with accountability for making sure all of those things are orchestrated. This combination of skills, high accountability, and attention to detail-oriented execution as well as macro-level strategy are the gifts that organizational leaders need. This is why the best product managers often graduate to senior management roles.

The role of a marketing campaign manager should be the proving ground for future CMOs. The campaign manager should care about every single element in a digital marketing campaign from its creative direction, to its analytics, to its financial performance, to the timeliness of its execution, to the measurement of its overall impact and success. And if you can handle that consistently, you might be a good CMO candidate.

But for some reason, this strategic marketing role does not exist widely in the current industry. The responsibility rests completely upon the CMO alone, it's outsourced to agencies and consultants, or worse, it just remains unaddressed.

CMOs should be responsible for answering high-level, strategic questions:

"Is our marketing working?"

"What is the value marketing has generated this year in layman's terms such as revenue, bookings, and pipeline?"

Who should be responsible for these critical campaign-level questions?

"Is this integrated campaign achieving our business goals?"

"Did the campaign return a compelling ROI?" (In other words, do we understand the financial value of the return, and can we compare it to the total campaign investment, all-in versus, say, cost per outcome or return on ad spend?)

"Looking across all our campaigns, which were more/less effective?"

"Can you describe campaign impact in terms the CEO and CFO understand (revenue, bookings, deals, churn reduction) instead of marketing-specialized metrics (click-through, downloads, impressions, reach)?"

"Why were different campaigns across diverse channel mixes more or less successful?"

Today, most teams are populated with staff that is focused on more tactical questions and measurements, using tools optimized to a specific channel. They can answer useful questions, but they can't answer these critical campaign-level questions that add tremendous value, not just to the marketing organization, but to the company.

Campaign managers can answer these questions. However, in a small company, CMOs handle them because they are the *de facto* marketing campaign managers, too. But as a company grows, a critical gap emerges.

Role description for a marketing campaign manager

A campaign manager is responsible for achieving the strategic goal of the campaign. It might be launching a new product, generating a certain number of sales-accepted leads, reducing churn by a certain percentage, or repositioning the company to grow revenue in a new marketing segment by a certain dollar amount. The outcome tends to be strategic and objectively measurable.

Campaign managers are responsible for rallying and administering the budget, staff, consultants, technology, channels, creative, and project management skills at their disposal to make it happen. They will know if things are on track, and have the ability to make course corrections as needed. They will be natural leaders with strong persuasion skills as well as analytical and financial aptitude. If it feels like a unicorn hire, then put the best fits in those roles, train them to close skills gaps, and build teams around them that possess complementary skills.

Marketing campaign managers are responsible for:

> **Audience:** Who are the people you're trying to reach? This could be named individuals, audience definition by job role (e.g., CIOs), by generation (e.g., Generation X), or a combination of characteristics (e.g., middle-income casual gamers, aged between 30 and 45, who own an Android phone).

Message: What are you going to say to your target audience? What is the message, or set of messages, you can craft to galvanize the desired outcome? The messaging does not live in a vacuum. It must be coordinated with your broader strategic narrative and be consistent with your branding, but it will be honed within that framework to achieve a target outcome.

Channel Mix: Channels are to marketing campaigns as packaging is to physical products. Like packaging, channels have very little inherent or stand-alone value, but when orchestrated with the other campaign elements they can make a significant impact on campaign performance.

Activities: What activities need to be undertaken, by whom, and when?

Investments: What are you going to spend on campaign execution? In principle, a high investment should yield larger outcomes than a low investment.

Measurement: What metrics will define the success of the campaign? Do you have the tools to measure them accurately and on the right cadence? Do they communicate business value, and preferably financial business value? If not, they may not be easy for people outside of marketing to appreciate.

By coordinating these elements within a marketing campaign, the campaign manager aims to drive the best possible outcomes. The relative importance of any of these elements varies by marketing campaign, but in all instances they operate together. They are the interlocking cogs in an engine—the campaign. Remove a cog and the engine won't work at all. Assemble the engine with well-fitted cogs working in perfect alignment and you have a winning campaign.

Audience, message, channels, activities, investments and measurement—these elements are conceptual peers. None is more important than the others, and all are interdependent. Ignore an element, and the campaign will fail. By that same token, if you overemphasize any element too strongly, the campaign will likely fail, too.

How channels killed marketing campaign management

Consider a few of the key marketing channels: TV, radio, print, OOH (Out of Home), digital, social media, and events. The tools, skills, consultants, platforms, reports, and all the things that are needed to orchestrate and run these campaigns are disparate. Unsurprisingly, individuals tend to become experts in executing campaigns over a subset of all the channels. Events managers rarely run digital campaigns as well, and vice versa. This leads to teams being structured around channel expertise, too.

Since budget allocations tend to follow team structure, many marketing teams allocate budget by channel. Furthermore, there are specialized, channel-specific tools, reports, and metrics for measuring performance in narrow ways that cannot possibly encompass everything that went into a campaign. For example, traditional ad platforms report ROI based entirely on ad spend, and don't capture any of the other costs that go into running and managing a digital marketing campaign such as SEO consultants and creative services costs.

In the previous section, we talked about the peer relationship between audience, messaging, channels, activities, investments, and measurement to organize a campaign. Yet, in a channel-oriented structure, we find investments and activities organized around channels. In such a team, individual performance is likely to be measured by the channel's performance. The individual is going to be focused, first and foremost, on the performance of that channel. He or she will want to preserve funds to be spent in that channel, and will need to be able to report analytically on how that channel is performing.

These are all good things to measure, but they are micro-level measurements. They do not tell the company whether its marketing campaigns are successful or not. They do not speak to which campaigns are more effective than others. Due to the channel-oriented structure and budget allocation in most organizations, the hierarchy in a channel-biased environment looks more like this:

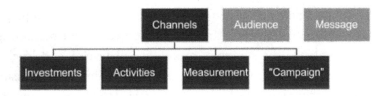

Channels have organizational dominance, and audience and messaging are relative afterthoughts. Or, the audience and the message are managed within the channel, leading to disparate strategies channel by channel. "Campaigns" are not true campaigns in this model. They are subordinate to the channel, which decreases the likelihood the campaign will achieve its goals, and hinders true campaign-level measurement. Such an orientation almost necessarily leads to a local approach to marketing measurement ("Which channels are performing best/worst?" and "Is social working?") rather than a global approach to marketing measurement ("Is this campaign achieving its target metrics and ROI?" and "Are we achieving our key goals?").

There is danger in thinking that the channel determines marketing success—it can only determine *marketing efficiency*. If the message is wrong for the target audience, if the audience reacts to the message in an undesirable way, it doesn't matter what channels you pick. If you have an attribution model that attributes value to some point in a customer journey (which we don't recommend, but if you do), don't forget to add this phrase, **"...for this particular message to this particular audience."** Otherwise, you may mistakenly think that it is the channel doing the heavy lifting rather than the complete blend of campaign elements. It only takes a moment's consideration to reaffirm that the success of a product launch is never primarily about the channel. It is about the campaign. It's time to reintroduce strategic marketing campaign management into organizations. Of course, it's unrealistic to expect marketing organizations to simply add staff. Or to tap into some imaginary latent market of people who have been patiently waiting on the sidelines with perfect campaign manager resumes. However, there is an opportunity for marketing teams to embrace the strategic importance of level 1 and level 2 measurement and to ensure they have representation in their team structures, technology stacks, and analytical landscape to answer the questions that pertain to those levels. Stretch your existing team members and help them learn new skills outside their channel specialization. Educate your team on the strategic marketing goals, and relentlessly repeat the goals. Help them see how their efforts impact the metrics that matter to the company.

Finally, ensure that each campaign (especially each multi-channel campaign) has a marketing campaign manager responsible for the audience, message, channels, activities, investments and measurement. He or she should also be responsible for the offer and the strategic campaign outcomes. Even if that is not a specialized and dedicated campaign manager, pick someone and make that individual accountable for the overall success of the program. Give that person authority and accountability for the campaign. Over time, the natural campaign managers (and future marketing leaders) will emerge, and your ability to consistently measure campaign performance will advance.

CHAPTER 5

Building a Winning Marketing Plan

As marketers we understand that a marketing plan is the most important and strategic document we will produce all year. The problem is we don't always treat it as such. For many of us, the urgent seems to get in the way of the important and we end up rushing to complete our plans at the end of the year to make deadlines aligned with executive team presentations. We often create the plans in silos with little input from sales or the product team. For those of you who have been with a company for more than a year, did you take the easy way out and use last year's plan to build out the current one? Be honest.

CMOs that have teams with more than 5 marketers usually have several functions to manage. The problem is that each of these functions are often focused on what they do well and not the greater goals. For this reason, marketing teams can have misaligned goals and campaigns tend to be function- or channel-specific rather than focused on the target audience and message. This dramatically impacts the effectiveness of a marketing plan.

Even when you have a plan, the team doesn't always follow it or know how to apply it to their function. How many times in the middle of a planning cycle have you heard an events person say, "I think we should run a dinner series" without any context to the plan or why? Or a digital marketer says, "Let's do an email campaign to the database" without thinking about segmentation or tying the activity to larger thematic campaigns outlined in the plan? These one-off tactical activities probably failed, or at least did not meet expectations. The question is, why?

There are five primary reasons why marketers run rudderless marketing activities and do not follow an established plan:

1. The plan that was built at the beginning of the year was not detailed enough for the team to use as a guide for their efforts

2. The team never fully understood how the marketing strategies fit with their roles, so they defaulted to what they know how to do instead of doing what aligns with the goals

3. The plan was solid, but it resides in a presentation deck somewhere, never to be seen again

4. Each member of the team built his or her own plan, which was never integrated across all the marketing functions

5. There wasn't a comprehensive, goals-driven plan

If there wasn't a plan in place, which unfortunately happens far too often, then there will most likely be a change in marketing leadership soon. All of the other scenarios listed above are direct failures of the CMO not setting a clear strategy, getting team buy-in, and continually reinforcing the direction by revisiting the plan.

To ensure you do not get caught in the busywork marketing cycle and are aligned with the marketing strategies, there are a series of questions you need to ask when new ideas, campaigns and programs come to light:

What is the goal we are trying to accomplish?
What is the right strategy to accomplish this goal?
Who is the target audience?
What are the messages we want to deliver to that target audience based on their needs?
Does this tie into a larger theme?
What are the success metrics?

If the answers align with the current plan and you are practicing an agile marketing approach, then you should consider the new initiative. But caution, if the conversation quickly gets tactical by starting with the marketing channel without providing answers consistent with your plan, think again.

What is a marketing plan?

Let's take a step back and talk about the definition of a marketing plan. In May 2021, *Wikipedia* offers the following:

> A **marketing plan** may be part of an overall business plan. Solid marketing strategy is the foundation of a well-written marketing plan so that goals may be achieved. While a marketing plan contains a list of actions, without a sound strategic foundation, it is of little use to a business.

This is problematic. When done correctly, there is no "*may* be part of an overall business plan," the marketing plan *is* a large portion of the business plan. And you need to think and prepare that way.

Organizations that sell to consumers (B2C) usually view marketing as the most strategic function at the company. For companies that sell to other businesses (B2B), marketing can be viewed as a support function for sales. In either case, the foundation for the marketing plan is the same: you need to identify the right buyer who has a need for your product, and you need to deliver a compelling message to inspire him or her to purchase.

Every comprehensive marketing plan should include the following strategic marketing elements—in this order—to build off each other:

1. Situational analysis (historical data)
2. Market research and analysis
3. Company goals
4. Marketing goals (these roll up to company goals)
5. Marketing strategies
6. Target audience (segmentation and need)
7. Positioning and messaging
8. Product and services direction and definition
9. Pricing and packaging
10. Competitive analysis
11. Sales channel strategy (distribution model, customer acquisition and lifetime value)
12. Sales support (messaging, training, tools)
13. Partner/channel strategy
14. Product and services launches
15. Campaigns
16. Marketing channels/vehicles (PR, trade shows, social, email, website, direct mail, etc.)
17. Programs
18. Marketing activity timeline/calendar
19. Marketing team structure/growth/responsibilities (org chart)
20. Technology (software)
21. Budget allocation
22. Testing (messages, ideas, markets)

23. Metrics of achievement

24. Assumptions, dependencies, risks

Unless you are the head of marketing or marketing operations, you may not be responsible for all these plan elements. However, every person plays a part in the success of the plan, so work with your team to carve out your role.

The Marketing Plan Framework

The following proposed **Marketing Plan Framework (MPF)** and template offers a definition for each plan element and examples of what to include in the plan:

Plan Element	Definition	Examples of What to Include
Situation analysis	Use learnings from the previous year and take current inventory of your company's status in the market. Look at historical data for performance and conduct a SWOT for a qualitative view of where you're at.	• SWOT analysis • Sales numbers • Lead gen numbers • Win/loss analysis • Marketing team skill set
Market research & analysis	The activity of gathering information about customer needs and preferences for analysis and decision making. Your marketing plan should combine your situation analysis and market research for goals and strategy decision making.	• Analyst report data • Competitive analysis • Independent surveys • Economic conditions • Expansion opportunities • Technology trends

Company goals	Business drivers that marketing goals will support. Most common company goals that pertain to marketing are related to sales, customers, or products/services.	• Revenue targets • Customer satisfaction • New products to market • Company perception
Marketing goals	Support the company goals. Create topline marketing goals—both qualitative and quantitative.	• See Goal Pyramid for a comprehensive list
Marketing strategies	Marketing strategy is a forward-looking approach and an overall game plan of any business. The purpose of the strategy is achieving a sustainable growth and competitive advantage. You can have different strategies for achieving different goals. In your marketing plan, build strategies for achieving each goal you set.	Examples of marketing strategies: • Growth • Promotional • Expansion (new markets) • Competitive replacement • Land and expand • Wedge issue • Product/services leadership • Customer retention/ loyalty • Content marketing • Viral marketing
Target audience (including segmentation and need)	Identify the ideal audience you would like to message in order to stimulate a response or create an impression.	• Target audience definition • Segmentation (by geo, demographics, behavioral, and psychographics) • Personas

Positioning and messaging	Positioning focuses your messaging platform. A positioning statement includes a target audience, the needs or wants of that target audience, your product or service definition, benefits of the offering, and differentiation from the competition. Supporting messages come from the positioning statement and should live in a messaging guide. The messaging guide provides consistency of message across different communications to multiple audiences. Both the positioning statement and topline messages should be in your plan.	Positioning statement: • Target audience • Need • Product definition • Benefits • Differentiators Messaging guide: • Company messaging • Product messaging • Messaging by audience • Competitive messaging • Messaging by channel • Customer requests
Product and services direction and definition	For companies that have brand management or product management as part of the marketing function, roadmap strategy will need to be part of the plan. It will be important to have a clear vision of what is coming to prepare for go-to-market launches.	Definition: • Clear articulation of the product value proposition Product direction: • Roadmap/innovation
Pricing and packaging	The process of finding the optimal price that the buyer is willing to pay for your products and services, taking profitability and the competition into account. Packaging creates product/ service configurations based on the target audience's needs. Both are essential elements of your marketing plan.	• Pricing table • Packages • Profitability analysis • Competitive pricing • Value/ROI analysis • Win/loss analysis

Competitive analysis	Competitive analysis is an assessment of the strengths and weaknesses of your competition. This evaluation provides both offensive and defensive strategic context to solidify differentiated competitive messaging.	• Full product/service analysis and comparison • Offensive messages • Defensive messages • Competitor 2x2 map
Sales channel strategy	Marketing's primary function is to drive sales to support the business, so outlining how the marketing strategy aligns with the sales strategy will be a critical element of the marketing plan.	• Sales model: direct vs. indirect sales channels • Sales team structure • Sales goals for the year • Lifetime customer value
Sales support	If the product you offer is complex or has a long evaluation cycle before a purchase, such as an automobile or enterprise software, it is important to have a sales support strategy and tactical execution plan. This will include sales training and tools to help them close business.	Training and sales tools: • Onboarding new salespeople • Sales skills training • Product & messaging training • Presentations, brochures, selling scripts, pricing tools
Partner/channel strategy	Partner strategy is a critical element of any marketing plan. Some companies sell direct to the buyer exclusively, but most have either a full indirect selling strategy or a mixture of both direct and indirect. For companies that sell indirect exclusively, this is their sales strategy.	• Partnering goals • Partner revenue targets • Partnering strategy • Partnering tactical plan • Partner program • Joint marketing programs

Product and services launches	Planning out product and services launches based on the roadmap will be a crucial part of the marketing plan. Product launches are one of the most important campaign types.	• Key messages • Announcement schedule • Communication strategy • Market education
Campaigns	Campaigns are large-scale marketing initiatives that are goals-based, have a specific target audience, promote a specific set of messages, use several communication channels, and can be measured. Campaigns are usually time-based. All campaigns should be included in the marketing plan. See campaigns template in chapter 7.	Examples of campaign types: • Integrated • Thematic • Promotional • Product launch • Demand generation • Thought leadership • Competitive replacement
Marketing channels (vehicles)	A marketing channel is a vehicle for carrying your key messages to the target audience. Marketing channels should be selected based on where their target audience goes, what they read, what they watch, and who they consult. There are a lot of offline and online marketing channels for reaching audiences so determining which ones have the greatest chance of reaching your target audience is critical for making a connection.	Examples of marketing channels: • Email • Social • Advertising - TV/radio/print • Trade shows/events • Search engine - SEM/SEO • Webinars • Content syndication • Website • Direct mail

Programs	Programs are ongoing initiatives that have goals and budget, but are not necessarily time-based or audience specific. Programs are not campaigns since many of the activities are created over the course of the year due to opportunistic marketing.	Program examples: • PR • Partner • Community • Loyalty • Social
Marketing activity timeline/ calendar	The marketing activity timeline has all the major milestones over the life of the plan. The timeline will include campaigns, launches, major events, etc. A more detailed project plan that includes the timeline will be created outside of your strategic marketing plan.	Milestone examples: • Product launches • Campaigns • Program launches • Expansion announcements • Major events
Marketing team structure, growth and responsibilities	A marketing team structure starts with the goals and what resources are necessary to achieve them. The plan must justify any new headcount and provide a structure for the new team members to be successful.	• Organizational chart • Scale requirements and resource justification • Division of team labor • Succession planning
Technology (software)	Include your current marketing technology stack and any additional systems you plan to add. Discuss any efficiency gains the technology will bring to the marketing team.	• Full tech stack • New tech implementation plan, timeline and payback • Expected efficiency gains

Budget allocation	Include a topline budget broken out by key functions, campaigns, and by time period. Budget is a critical part of the process and necessary in order to successfully execute your plan. Build your plan first, and mandate the funds you need to achieve the goals.	• Headcount • Discretionary spend • Technology spend • Correlate budget to sales performance for true ROI
Testing	Testing takes several forms. Using a test market is a good way to gather data on a certain demographic or geo to gauge product/service interest prior to roll-out. A/B testing is a method of determining buyer preferences by comparing messages. Surveys and focus groups can also help gather valuable input to improve marketing effectiveness.	• Test market • A/B testing • Surveys • Focus groups • Independent research
Metrics of achievement	Measurement of critical goal-based success metrics that represent marketing performance. Most marketing metrics are indicators of sales performance and should be measured in terms of return on investment.	• Impressions • Leads • Influenced pipeline • Opportunities • Sales • Conversion rate • Lifetime value • Customer satisfaction • Market share

| Assumptions, dependencies and risks to success | Now that you have your plan, include a list of assumptions that are essential for success and the dependencies your team will require to be effective. Understand the key internal and external risks to the successful execution of the marketing plan. Lastly include scenario planning to prepare best case and worst-case scenarios. | • Budget
• Sales team readiness
• Product roadmap delivery
• Industry dynamics
• Economic dynamics
• Competitive pressure
• Staffing/talent challenges
• Budget cut risk
• Organizational commitment
• Cross-functional cooperation |

It might look like a daunting task to think through all of the elements of the marketing plan list above. But, if you build the plan in collaboration with your marketing team, collectively everyone will be focused on what is important instead of marketing in silos. Planning is the first step toward becoming an agile marketer.

Marketing Plan Approaches

Before you start building your marketing plan you need to select an approach. There are three primary approaches:

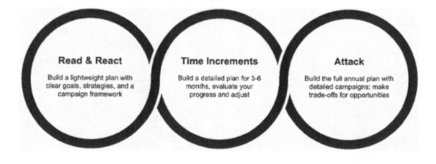

Read and React: A read and react planning approach allows for the most flexibility but it also requires discipline. The marketing team builds a lightweight plan (essentially an outline) with a solid set of clear goals and strategies. The team meets weekly to determine what needs to be done in order to achieve the goals. The benefit is the team is nimble and can react to any changes in the business without having to follow a fully-baked plan. This approach requires a seasoned team that is very organized and likes to innovate. The downside of this approach is that the team will inevitably waste time ideating everything on the fly.

Time Increments: This approach bridges the other two, by combining planning in small time increments with constantly reevaluating the plan throughout the year. The only issue with this approach is that planning cycles can sneak up on teams—and when they do, they require significant work. This approach can be used with a team that has a blend of both experienced and junior resources.

Attack: An attack approach requires full annual planning. The benefit is that this approach maximizes efficiency; there is no ambiguity as to what a team needs to work on next. The downsides are that it requires months of work to build out, and it renders teams less nimble when required changes occur. This approach is good to use with a junior marketing team since it keeps everyone focused on what's coming up next.

When choosing a planning approach, first understand your team's level of experience and the group dynamics. Know your workload and assess how much time you have to spend on your plan. Lastly, take into account the amount of change happening at your company and in your industry; if it's significant, you might need an agile marketing plan.

Building an Agile Marketing Plan

Let's say you and your team have just built the best plan ever using the Marketing Plan Framework (MPF). The plan fully aligns with the goals as they stand today and details a comprehensive strategy for achieving them. You start executing the plan to perfection and then, out of nowhere, the roadblocks to success start to appear. Before you know it, you are off course.

The list of reasons why your plan can crumble is long. Below are some common causes:

1. Economic volatility causes budget cuts
2. Competition comes out with a new and improved product or revised pricing
3. You have employee turnover of key marketers on your team
4. Your plan isn't achieving the stated goals
5. The sales team is not prepared to do its part
6. The CEO changes the company direction
7. The R&D team does not hit its release dates
8. The industry you sell to starts drying up
9. You fail to get traction in a new geographic location
10. You have to overspend on a campaign, so you need to modify the plan
11. The team does not understand, or buy into, the plan
12. You hire the wrong skill set or onboard someone late, creating a capacity gap
13. New hires don't pan out, leaving you shorthanded

14. Vendors you hire don't understand the plan and have misaligned output
15. The sales team decides to take a different approach or direction
16. Your partners do not hold up their end of the bargain
17. Lead generation emergencies arise and distract the team
18. Campaigns and programs get delayed creating a ripple effect downstream
19. Major marketing events get cancelled
20. Marketing leadership changes

How many of these have you experienced? Hopefully this list did not send a chill up your spine, but these are the key contributors as to why CMOs have the shortest lifespan in the C-suite. So what does this mean? It means you need to build a plan that is flexible and prepares for different scenarios. In other words, you need to build an agile marketing plan.

Why do you need to be agile? Because stuff happens—both good and bad. In either case, your plan can get back-burnered while full effort is put toward taking advantage of the new opportunity or resolving the current issue at hand. All too often, after the disruption subsides, the plan is derailed, and the team engages in rudderless marketing activities hoping that something works. The problem is, hope is not a strategy. More often than not, this only results in unachieved goals.

An agile marketing plan is made up of three key components:

1. Flexing for opportunistic marketing
2. Underachievement scenario planning
3. Overachievement scenario planning

Flexing for Opportunistic Marketing

Depending on your company size, numerous unplanned opportunities will emerge over the course of the year—a customer wants to do a press release with you, an industry analyst ranks your product or service the best on the planet, or a partner wants to OEM your product and do joint marketing.

In marketing, you are constantly working with the outside world. The problem is that you can't control what these external audiences do or the timing of the opportunities they place at your feet. You can only control your end of the equation.

Typically, there are three reasons you pass on unplanned opportunities: timing, resources, and budget. But if you have that information at your fingertips, then you can quickly compare a new opportunity against the current plan to determine which will have more impact on the goals. The key steps to the evaluation process are:

Assess if the opportunity helps to achieve the annual marketing goals and is executable

Prioritize by comparing new opportunities against existing marketing campaigns

Collaborate with the team to plan for new opportunities and modify existing campaigns

Reallocate funds accurately without going over budget

Execute the new campaign in the context of the original plan and track performance

A word of caution: Don't let frequent "urgent opportunities" distract you from the original goals-based plan, but be flexible if the opportunity is too good to pass up.

Planning for Under- and Overachievement

When building an agile marketing plan, start with your baseline plan (the one that was built to achieve the original company objectives) and use it as a barometer to build your scenarios— these are a set of restated goals, either higher or lower, determined by business outcomes that deviate significantly from the original objectives. These scenario-based goals have a material impact on the marketing plan's strategy, campaigns, and budget. The purpose of scenario planning is so that when you recognize changes in the business, you have a pre-built plan to quickly course correct.

When creating scenarios, the first step is to define a new set of goals based on under- or overperformance. Once the objectives are established, create a set of goal based scenarios that are triggered by pre-defined thresholds. These scenarios are designed to either prepare you for dealing with bumps in the road that cause underperformance, or leverage overperformance to supercharge your marketing.

For underachievement, it's not necessary to create more than one scenario, but having two [slight underachievement (25%) and significant underachievement (50%)] is recommended if your business has variability or ambitious goals. If you feel there is a chance underachievement could be greater than 50%, you may want to redo your original plan. Companies with this level of variability are usually start-ups or businesses with little to no historical data.

For conservative marketing plans with potential revenue upside, you might want to also look at an overachievement scenario. When building this, check with the CFO to confirm that if revenue targets are exceeded, marketing will receive some of the proceeds for additional programs. Ideally you will want to leverage the newly acquired funds (house money) to conduct experiential marketing initiatives aimed at expanding your current repertoire of campaigns and programs.

There is a seven-step process for building and executing scenarios:

1. Identify the driving forces behind the potential risks, issues, or decisions
2. Determine the impact to the current goals
3. Create a new set of goals that map to underachievement or overachievement
4. Rank the strategies, campaigns and programs by criticality (highest impact to the business), keeping in mind budget thresholds (especially in case of cuts)
    a. Align the ranked marketing initiatives to the scenarios based on severity (higher or lower)
    b. Assign a numerical ranking or categorization such as "keep, consider, or cut"
5. Build a tiered structure based on the level of under- or overachievement
6. Select metrics for monitoring and create thresholds for when scenarios are triggered
7. Assess the impact of switching to the scenario and adjust accordingly to alternative strategies

Alternative strategies for overachievement are limitless, but when you underachieve, human and financial resources usually get tight. There are some inexpensive marketing options to explore if you have to put together an underachievement plan. Switching from paid to free marketing is the best place to start. Strategies such as content, social, viral, word of mouth, and joint marketing with partners (splitting the expenses) can be very cost effective and will stretch your discretionary spend. If the cuts are primarily to headcount, reallocating financial resources to AI-related marketing software can create lots of efficiencies across the board. You can also look at cheaper offshore vendors for activities such as design, SEM, and telemarketing.

CHAPTER 6

Goals-Based Marketing

Marketing is one of the most strategic functions of a company—when executed correctly. In a perfect world, marketing defines products and services, the target audience, messaging, competitive positioning, distribution channels, communication vehicles, and how the products and services are priced and packaged. For this reason, creating a strategy and tactics without first carefully and clearly defining a set of goals that align with company initiatives is a risky proposition that could negatively impact the overall business.

If we as marketers are honest with ourselves, the process of building and managing a marketing plan is rarely smooth sailing. Usually, we receive the company objectives from the executive team and the budget number from finance and we back into the marketing plan. Letting others at your organization dictate the terms of how you will go to market, without any input from you on what success looks like, will not help you achieve operational marketing excellence.

Another common pitfall that happens too often: months after you finalize your marketing plan and budget and begin executing, the company direction changes. As nimble marketers, we flex to execute a new set of tactical requirements (most likely lead generation) to solve the urgent problem thrust upon us. But, do we revisit the original plan and budget we created? It's most likely lost in a slide deck or spreadsheet, right? Do we modify or reset the goals when changes arise so there is visibility, continuity, and consistency across the team? Unfortunately, the answers are often "no." The original plan quickly becomes irrelevant and the age-old tradition of aimless, busy-work marketing ensues.

There are six primary reasons marketers lose sight of their goals:

1. Missing revenue targets creates desperate marketing activities to fill the pipeline
2. The management team regularly changes priorities or is unaligned, creating confusion
3. Team turnover, especially in leadership, hurts continuity across different functions
4. A tactically-focused junior team didn't understand the goals in the first place
5. The marketing plan was misaligned with the stated goals, or worse, was built without goals
6. The goals are collecting dust in a slide deck delivered at the beginning of the year

Since most marketing teams are made up of different functions, team members may have their own unique methods for managing the plan and budget. This by nature will create inconsistencies in how the different functions on the marketing team interpret the best way to achieve the stated goals. In addition, team members may have different processes and communication vehicles for the goals, resulting in a lack of visibility and accountability. This limited visibility of the goals will cause marketers to create tactical, rudderless campaigns and programs, which result in spending on the wrong activities and creating budget risk.

Further complicating things, budgeting is typically a finance activity with too much emphasis on how much is spent versus highlighting the value of what each monetary line item represents toward achieving the marketing goals. Typically, the finance team provides marketing with a budget number at the beginning of the year and forces them to build a plan from it. This guesswork approach is backwards—the goals and plan need to come first. It also puts pressure on the marketing team to spend the full budget, even if it's not necessary to achieve the goals. It is wasteful, empty-calorie marketing if the budget is not aligned with achieving the stated goals.

How to define goals

Defining goals can be very easy or complicated depending on the stage of your company. Companies that are smaller may have more to accomplish, but they have fewer resources to achieve and track a broad set of goals. For larger established companies, the goals may be clearer, but with a large team comes a variety of individual goals that must support marketing initiatives and company objectives.

In any case, the first step in the process is to get executive team alignment on the company objectives. Marketing will most likely have a significant role in achieving many of the company objectives, so it's critical that plans and budgets are created with the goals in mind. In order to ensure this is carried out, you must also get buy-in from the full marketing team on topline goals, so everyone is marching in the same direction. Without executive alignment and marketing team buy-in on the goals, confusion on strategy and tactics will follow.

When establishing what you need to achieve for the upcoming year, remember not all goals can be accurately measured. For this reason, marketers should feel comfortable using a mixture of both quantitative (x number of leads) and qualitative (rebrand the company) goals.

Whether you work for a large company or a small one, all goals can be consolidated into three topline marketing objectives:

Sales (maintaining or expanding the business)
Awareness (getting the word out)
Perception (manage the brand, positioning, and messaging)

Try to come up with a marketing goal that does not fit into one of these objectives. You may find one, such a product launch, that could help achieve all three of these topline objectives, but it always comes back to these three. Below is a chart containing examples of commonly used goals demonstrating how neatly they fit under these top-level objectives.

After defining your qualitative goals, you will be ready to build your marketing strategy to achieve them. Ensure your marketing budget is sufficient enough to achieve each goal and build a set of campaigns that are designed to optimize performance against the goal. Ideally, your goals, plan, campaigns, programs, activities, budget and performance metrics should all be kept in the same place, so they can be interconnected and visible at all times for collaboration.

Lastly, ask yourself how much time you put into creating the goals. If the answer is less than 10 minutes (be honest), then you are most likely not setting optimized or achievable goals.

Topline Objectives	Qualitative Goals
Sales	Acquire new customers
	Create opportunities
	Generate leads
	Grow market share through competitive replacement
	Upsell/cross-sell customers
	Build new sales channels
	Expand into new markets (by geo, demo, industry, size)
	Optimize pricing against the competition
	Retain customers
Awareness	Create website traffic
	Generate social buzz
	Get more PR coverage
	Build an industry analyst program
	Announce partner program or sales channels
	Launch new product/service/solution/community/company
	Market expansion
Perception	Rebrand the company and products
	Reposition the company
	Refine/change messaging
	Build a content marketing program
	Become a thought leader
	Competitive differentiation
	Increase customer satisfaction

Setting realistic goals

Marketers don't take goals as seriously as they should. This most likely stems from the fact that marketing has been an inexact science until a decade ago. Since it was tough to prove success back in the day, goals were more arbitrary or qualitative in nature and limited in their ability to demonstrate clear return on investment (ROI). Below are some common reasons why marketers end up with unrealistic goals:

> **Data gap:** No relevant historical data, resulting in "best guess" goals

> **Executive pressure:** Doing what the Board/CEO wants

> **Hero complex:** CMO takes on too much responsibility for achieving the company goals

> **Resource imbalance:** Available human and financial resources are not taken into account

> **No strategy alignment:** There isn't a clear strategy with campaigns to achieve goals

> **No team alignment:** Team member are not assigned sub-goals that roll-up to help achieve topline objectives (resulting in wasted resources)

Over the last decade the game has changed due to digital transformation, which has provided marketers with better performance tracking and visibility. Finally, they can measure most of their marketing success with the same level of detail as the sales and finance teams. But since marketing ultimately has a more diverse set of responsibilities, it is essential to build a goals-based structure that everyone on the team maps to.

Getting started: creating your goals

First, start early. You should set your goals for the following year six months in advance, but be nimble in case any major market, competitor, or company changes emerge and significantly impact your objectives.

Before you build a plan or set your budget, clearly define your goals. Make sure you engage in a scenario-planning exercise to determine a best- versus worst-case view of your performance against the goals. Use that same scenario-based philosophy when you start building your plan and creating campaigns.

Depending on the size and sophistication of your team, you want to keep the number of annual goals under nine, with an optimal range between four to six. Too many goals will spread a marketing team's focus too thin, making it harder for goals to be achieved.

When setting the goals, take into account the following:

Company goals: Always start with the company goals for organizational alignment. Determine the goals where marketing can have the biggest impact and set your metrics of achievement accordingly.

Historical data: Review your historical numbers and look for patterns and trends that could give you an indication of future results. If the trends do not align with your stated goals, then you will need to either reset expectations or increase investment.

Marketing team: When evaluating your team's ability to achieve the goals, ask the following questions: Does your team structure have functional gaps? Are there team members with limited skill sets? Do you have enough productive people with bandwidth? You will not achieve your goals unless you have the right team, period. Any gaps need to be filled in a timely fashion, either through hiring new employees or through outsourced staff, otherwise you risk missing your deadlines for hitting your goals.

Marketing budget: Set your goals and build your plan, then go to finance and fight for the budget. Don't let finance tell you what the budget is—work with them to get what you need in order to achieve the goals.

The competition: Too often we only think about the competition when it comes to market share goals. The competition needs to factor into all your decisions since there will be competitive reactions to every strategy your company undertakes. If your competition is successful in blocking you, it will make achieving your goals difficult.

Market conditions: If you're heading into a period of economic unrest without a recession-proof product or service, you need to take these economic factors into account. This is where scenario planning can help you be ready for any situation, so you can course correct.

Your sales function: Marketers need to take a critical look at the sales team and ask the tough questions before setting goals. Is the sales team set up with business development representatives (BDRs), geographical distribution, sales training, etc. to support your marketing goals? Can the sales team grow fast enough to handle the demand generated by marketing? Is finding talent a problem? Does your company have a great onboarding process, or does it take a long time for sales reps to get up to speed? Since sales and marketing go hand in hand, these questions will help you gauge how aggressively to set your goals.

Your product/service: Sometimes products and services do not come out on the expected launch date and marketing is left hanging. When tuning your goals, ask these two essential questions: Does your product/services team have a solid track record of on-time delivery? Do they have a history of great quality? If the answer to both is "yes," then you can set your goals accordingly.

Creating a Goals Pyramid

High-level objectives with no supporting goals will not yield results. For this reason, you need to make sure your whole team understands their roles in achieving the goals. Next, when creating the strategy, ensure it is aligned with achieving the goals. Lastly, make sure your campaigns are all goals-based. The best way to create this type of structure, visibility, and accountability is to build a Goals Pyramid.

A Goals Pyramid pulls all your strategic marketing together to provide clear direction to the team. The Pyramid starts with your topline marketing objectives which are matched up with more specific qualitative goals, metrics, and strategies to achieve the objectives. Here's a more in-depth look at what it contains:

Topline objectives: As you read earlier in this chapter, almost all marketing goals fall into one of three topline objectives: sales, awareness, or perception. This is why they are at the top of the Goals Pyramid. They help structure all the rest of your thinking as you start the marketing planning process.

Qualitative goals: These are more descriptive and customized to your unique business needs. In our example below, a qualitative goal of "generate opportunities" provides more color to the topline goal of "sales."

Metrics of achievement: These are the quantifiable goals that provide specific measurement to the qualitative goals. In our example Pyramid, we have written "generate 400 opportunities."

Team/individual sub-goals: These are metrics-based sub-goals the team or an individual needs to achieve. In our example, the digital marketing team needs to create 250 of the 400 opportunities next year.

Marketing strategy: This is the strategy you're using to achieve the goal. In the example below, the digital marketing team is using a "digital advertising strategy" to reach the target audience and generate the 250 opportunities.

Campaigns: All your campaigns should be goals-based, no matter how big or small. The campaigns will leverage the strategy and will aim to achieve the goal metrics. In our example, the campaign will promote a free trial in order to reach the goal of 250 opportunities.

Topline objectives
Sales

Qualitative goals
Generate opportunities

Metrics of achievement
400 opportunities

Team and individual goals
Digital Marketing
team - 250 opportunities

Marketing strategies
Digital Advertising

Campaigns
Free trial

GOALS PYRAMID

If you use the Goals Pyramid method, your team will always stay focused on what really matters and you will avoid empty calorie marketing.

Getting your marketing team onboard

Today, many companies are refactoring their goals due to volatile market conditions. When this happens, goals-based marketing plans can get complex fairly quickly, especially if you are creating both qualitative and quantitative goals that are multifactorial. Make certain your team understands the updated goals at an intimate level, especially the ones that are relevant to their functional area. Some best practices include:

1. Collaborating with the full team on setting objectives
2. Making goal creation your first strategic activity (before building the plan)
3. Assigning each team member individual goals that support hitting the topline objectives
4. Implementing weekly status reports that focus on activity to achieve the goals
5. Building scenario-based goals and strategies so everyone can quickly adapt to changes in the market landscape or new corporate initiatives
6. Creating one location where the goals, strategy, campaigns, and budget all reside so the team can find them and have a constant reminder of what's important

Number six on the list above looks simple and logical, but is a common mistake made by many marketing teams. Too often the goals live in a slide presentation, the strategy in another document, and the campaigns are in a spreadsheet—all disconnected. The process for strategy and plan implementation must be built in a way so that the marketing team never loses sight of the goals, always keeping them front and center for all activities. The only way this works is when the goals and the plan are consolidated for easy collaboration and modification by team members.

Next: A corresponding marketing strategy

Now that you have all your goals set for the year and buy-in from the entire marketing team, you need to build a strategy for achieving each goal. The strategies you create will be the essence of your marketing plan and should be used to shape your campaigns. When building your strategy, you must keep in mind achieving your topline objectives, qualitative goals, and measurable metrics of achievement or you risk not delivering on what matters most.

Here is an example of a marketing strategy in the context of the Goals Pyramid structure:

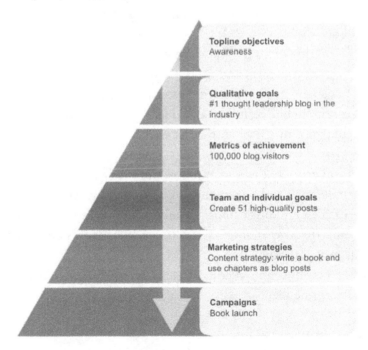

Topline objectives
Awareness

Qualitative goals
#1 thought leadership blog in the industry

Metrics of achievement
100,000 blog visitors

Team and individual goals
Create 51 high-quality posts

Marketing strategies
Content strategy: write a book and use chapters as blog posts

Campaigns
Book launch

The topline objective in this example is to create awareness for the company. The qualitative goal of becoming the #1 thought leadership blog in the industry in terms of readership adds specificity to the type of awareness and provides a target for the team. In order to reach the lofty metric of achievement set at 100,000 blog visitors, the marketing team knows the content needs to be outstanding so that word spreads. Although using a content marketing strategy seems straightforward, the real question is, how do you do it well and efficiently?

The marketing strategy chosen for this example is to write a book and segment the chapters into a blog post series. The marketing team estimates if they write 10 chapters and divide them into five blog posts each, they will generate 50 high-quality blog posts that count toward achieving their team goal of 51 thought-provoking posts for the year. By breaking up the book content into a series, they can entice readers to come back the following week to learn more about the topic.

This marketing strategy also spawns a book launch campaign to further create awareness and drive visitors back to the blog. As part of the book launch campaign, different marketing channels such as social media, public relations, and digital will be used to guide the target audience to the blog, further ensuring success of the stated goals.

As you can see, the marketing strategy is the connective tissue between the goals and campaigns. Thinking through your marketing strategy makes building campaigns easier and provides the "how" for your team. If you are not doing this today, include this best practice in your next planning cycle.

When creating a marketing strategy to achieve goals, marketers must determine the:

1. Audiences to target
2. Messages that resonate with the audience
3. Campaign or series of campaigns
4. Set of marketing channels/vehicles to reach the target audience
5. Marketing cadence (blast, pulse, drumbeat, etc.)

6. Amount of budget to allocate for supporting the cadence
7. Time frame
8. Owner of the strategy in order to achieve the goal

After you determine these eight elements, they become the cornerstone of your marketing plan.

Measuring goals based on the proper success metric

At the end of the day, goals are only good if you can measure them accurately. Although we have come a long way, measurement these days has still not hit the level of perfection we all desire. Qualitative goals can be tricky to measure. For this reason, we've listed some below, and coupled them with the best way to measure success. The qualitative goals are grouped by the topline objectives they serve, as illustrated in the Goals Pyramid diagram.

Goal	How to Measure Success
Sales	
Acquire new customers	Count # of new customers
Reduce customer churn	% of customers that stay vs. those that leave
Increase revenue	Count overall revenue growth over prior period
Upsell/cross-sell customers	Count marketing-sourced upsell/cross-sells
Create marketing-sourced revenue	Count the revenue originated by marketing
Create marketing-influenced revenue	Count the revenue influenced by marketing
Create marketing-sourced opportunities	Count # of opportunities created by marketing

Generate marketing-sourced leads	Count the # of leads created by marketing
Build/grow a contact database	Count the # of contacts
Grow a new sales channel	Count indirect channel revenue
Reduce sales cycle time	Average time of all deals from lead to close
Grow market share through competitive replacement	% Determined by survey or reported revenue
Expand into new markets (by geo, demo, industry, size)	Count # of customers
Retain customers	Customer retention %

Awareness

Improve awareness	Count impressions, articles, social mentions, etc.
Increase web traffic	Count the # of visitors on your website
Launch a new initiative	Count # of mentions, social shares, web visitors
Launch a new product or solution	Count # of mentions, social shares, web visitors
Educate external audiences	Downloads/views of content
Generate social followers	Count the # followers
Get more news coverage (PR)	Count the articles
Grow share of voice	Percent of articles you generate vs. competition
Create more speaking opportunities	Count the # of opportunities and the attendance
Build an industry analyst program	Count the # of mentions by analysts
Grow content marketing program	Count the # of pieces of content

Perception

Increase customer satisfaction	Target score, Net Promoter Score (NPS), survey
Increase customer evangelism	Count the # of case studies, speaking opps. etc.
Rebrand or re-position	Positive feedback from focus group or survey
Refine/change messaging	Measure online or email click-through rates
Optimize pricing against the competition	# of customer wins against the competition
Segment the customer base	Track interest in segmented content (i.e. website)
Launch partner program	Count the # of partners that join
Launch new product/service/ community/company	Measure awareness over time via survey
Become a thought leader	Count the number of content views

Goals are a critical part of marketing planning, campaigns, budget management, and performance measurement. Assign goals to everything you do in marketing, and you will not only be able to justify your investment of time and money, but you'll be able to track your success.

CHAPTER 7

Defining, Creating, & Applying Marketing Strategy

Defining Marketing Strategy

The term "marketing strategy" is thrown around liberally these days to the point that it now represents anything in marketing that is not tactical. It is a term that makes marketers feel smart when they say it (which inspires the frequent use of it in conversation). Think about it, how often have you heard marketers say things like, "We're building a marketing strategy for this year," with no real clarity as to what that is. The issue with the term "marketing strategy" is that the meaning has gotten so broad that very few people can actually define it. If this is the case, then what is marketing strategy?

Below is how *Wikipedia* defines marketing strategy:

> **Marketing strategy** is a long-term, forward-looking approach and an overall game plan of any organization or any business with the fundamental goal of achieving a sustainable competitive

advantage by understanding the needs and wants of customers.

Scholars like Philip Kotler continue to **debate** the precise meaning of marketing strategy. Consequently, the literature offers many different definitions. On close examination, however, these definitions appear to centre around the notion that strategy refers to a broad statement of what is to be achieved.

- *Wikipedia,* March 25, 2021

Well, that definition was as clear as mud. With all the experienced marketers and scholars that contribute to *Wikipedia*, it's alarming that they are still debating the meaning of the term. That said, it has not stopped marketers from using the phrase "marketing strategy" in conversation ad nauseam.

So, what is "marketing strategy"? Simply put, it's **the approach marketers take to achieve a goal**. The truth is that marketing strategy is not one comprehensive approach; there are many strategies that marketers deploy over the course of the year to achieve their objectives. Strategies serve as the connective tissue between goals and campaigns—they should always map to a goal and steer the development of marketing campaigns.

To illustrate this point, see the diagram below:

- Marketing goals support achieving company goals
- **Marketing strategies align with achieving marketing goals**
- **Campaigns leverage the marketing strategies**
- Channels execute the marketing campaigns

Think of a marketing strategy as the GPS that guides marketers as they determine the right approach for optimizing campaigns and tactics to achieve a goal. Without creating and deploying strategies, building campaigns can be challenging. Some marketers create strategies instinctively and it becomes an organic part of their marketing planning process. Unfortunately, today too many marketers are focused exclusively on marketing channel execution. They start their planning with the marketing channel (usually the one they are responsible for, since marketing has become so siloed) and then retrofit messaging, goals, and metrics.

How many times have you heard a marketer say, "Let's do an email campaign." This results in the team executing random acts of marketing and hoping for the best outcome. But as you know, "hope is not a strategy, and in the world of marketing, this is no exception.

When determining the right strategy, the process needs to originate with an understanding of the goals, and then map strategies to the goals before creating campaigns and selecting the channels. Marketing execution will usually fall short when it does not leverage the insight and guidance a strategy provides for applying the right approach in order to achieve a goal. Let's use the example from the Goals Pyramid, to more closely examine the way a strategy connects the dots:

Company X has a topline goal: become the market leader in their industry. To contribute to the company objective of leadership, the marketing team sets a goal to become the thought leader in the industry. Marketing applies a content marketing strategy to achieve their thought leadership goal. They select an eBook as the ideal content asset for communicating their deep understanding of the industry. Lastly, the team develops a campaign for launching and promoting the eBook using a variety of communication channels (email, social, website, advertising, content syndication, etc.) to reach the target audience.

The graphic below illustrates the thought process for this content strategy example:

Now let's take a look at a business-to-consumer (B2C) example:

Retailer Y has a company goal to grow sales for the year. The marketing team sets a goal to drive more store traffic. The strategy they select is a promotional one. Retailer Y built a "buy one, get one" (BOGO) campaign to bring customers into their retail outlets using a diverse set of marketing channels to communicate the promotion.

- Drive more traffic supports the grow sales goal

- **Promotional strategy aligns with the drive store traffic goal**

- **BOGO campaign is the execution of the promotional strategy**

- Channels execute the marketing campaigns

There are different strategies for achieving the multitude of goals marketers set each year in their marketing plan. You can also use multiple strategies to achieve different elements of a singular ambitious goal. An example of this is a goal almost all companies have—sales growth. There are many marketing goals, and subsequent strategies, that will help a company grow the topline:

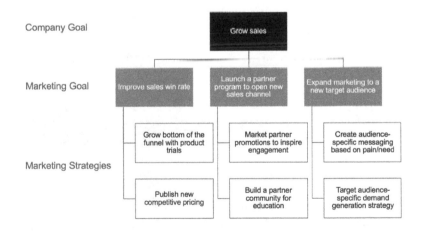

Marketers can now build their campaigns by leveraging each of these strategies. The number of campaigns a company should run per strategy could simply be one. There is no exact science as to whether or not a strategy requires multiple campaigns to help achieve a goal. Below are two examples, the first showing a single campaign approach and the second showing a more comprehensive approach.

Single campaign example

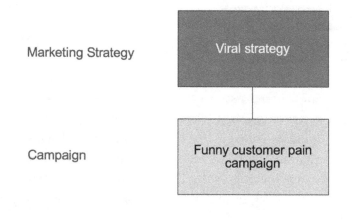

Multi-campaign example

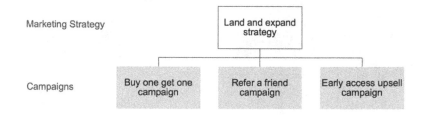

Some campaigns are so large that they may incorporate several strategies. An example of this is a product launch. A product launch campaign can be so broad that it can contribute to the achievement of several goals such as awareness, product perception, and sales growth.

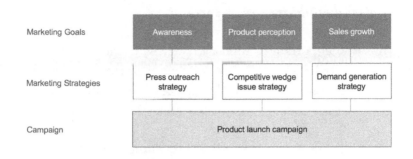

To help you better understand the multitude of strategies available, included below are some examples of commonly used marketing strategies arranged by the goal they are designed to achieve. This is not a comprehensive list since there are hundreds of strategies a marketer can use. You may have even used some of these strategies in the past without ever defining them or writing them down.

Strategy Template for Selecting the Right Strategy to Achieve a Goal	
Proposed strategy	Choose a strategy to achieve the goal
Strategy success factors	Evaluation criteria for determining strategy viability
Team	Evaluate the team (experienced, average, junior)
Budget	Estimate the budget (high, medium, low)
Complexity	Determine the complexity (high, medium, low)
Target audience	Define the audience (prospect, customer, partner, press, analyst, etc.)
Competition	Research the competition (differentiation, pricing, etc.)
Industry	Learn the industry (regulated vs. unregulated)
Region	Discover the region (cultural differences, regulations, holidays, etc.)
Product/service fit	Define the product or service (complex vs. simple)
Timeline	Estimate the time it will take to execute (base it on the goal timeline)
Historical data	Analyze the data (level of achievement, room for improvement)
Expected ROI	Calculate the potential ROI (revenue, contribution margin)

Why is marketing strategy important?

If it is so important to align a strategy with a goal, why doesn't every marketer create them when building their marketing plan?

There are several reasons why marketers gravitate toward the tactics rather than taking a goal-based strategy approach, including:

- The pressure to generate leads forces marketers into execution mode
- Creating strategies requires effort and can be difficult to ideate
- Many marketers start their careers in tactical jobs and never get exposed to strategies
- Marketing roles have become siloed, creating a narrow view of what is important
- Some marketing organizations don't have goals
- The MarTech software tools that have been created to date focus on the tactics

If this is the case, how does a marketing organization become more strategic? The answer is simple: start with your goals. When you have a goal you must achieve, it will force you to figure out how best to achieve it. Even if the CEO has not given you a set of goals, create them yourself so you have a guide that will unite the marketing team and help you measure your performance.

Building Your Strategies

Once you have identified the goals you are looking to accomplish, it's time to create your strategies to fulfill the objectives. To identify the right strategies, you first need to take into account the following factors:

Marketing team: The size, experience, and level of innovation your team possesses are all factors in selecting a marketing strategy. If you have an innovative team with deep experience, then you will have an opportunity to select from a wider range of strategies. Some strategies require a lot of effort and time to execute, and if you don't have the horsepower to execute them, you could miss your target dates or suffer quality issues.

Budget: Since a strategy is guiding the tactics of your marketing, budget is a key factor in the strategy's viability. Some strategies can be expensive to execute. Additionally, if your team lacks the experience to execute a strategy, you can apply budget toward outside resources, but this could result in a costly strategy that yields a negative ROI. You need to think through strategy execution to identify the areas of cost before you select it.

Complexity: Some strategies are very complex and require other teams at the company (outside of marketing) to support them. A big announcement strategy is an example of a situation where other groups within a company must contribute components like product, expertise, or funds. Complexity can tax an inexperienced team as well as your budget, so it's imperative to determine that the strategy is the right one to achieve your goal.

Target audience: Strategies almost always have a specific target audience. For this reason, strategies are unlikely to be interchangeable between audiences.

For an extreme example, you may not want to use a refer-a-friend strategy if the product you're marketing is personal in nature to the customer.

Competition: Examine the strategies your competition is using. It's difficult to come up with something in marketing that's truly unique, so borrowing a successful strategy is common. However, if you are focusing on differentiation from the competition, then you will want to use a unique strategy.

Industry: Certain industries have regulations where specific strategies will not work. Some can't accept gifts, some have strong security stances, and some have privacy rules. Take regulations into consideration when selecting a strategy.

Region: Cultural differences and regulatory issues like General Data Protection Regulation (GDPR) will limit what you can do in certain regions of the world. That said, other regions have cultural norms that open up an opportunity for a more diverse set of strategies. If your strategy is global, you need to consider these factors.

Product/service fit: Today, the products and services sold across many industries are diverse with different price points, sales cycle times, distribution channels, and buyer personas. Keep this diversity in mind as you set your strategies because the best option might be a strategy that is not a natural fit for your industry—for example, using a promotional strategy in B2B marketing. Sometimes an approach like this can work. Conversely, there are strategies that will not work in certain situations such as using a trial strategy if your product is difficult to understand.

Timeline: Can you execute the strategy in time to achieve the goal it aligns with? Marketing as a profession allows for a ton of creativity, and sometimes we get caught up in our own brilliance. In certain instances, you need to be practical. If the strategy is going to take longer than the required time frame, then it should be abandoned immediately. Remember strategies are built to achieve a goal, and all goals have timelines to measure success.

Historical data: If you have used a specific strategy in the past, then it is important to collect data to measure if it was successful. That will help you make the decision about whether or not to use the strategy. The definition of insanity is to do the same thing over and over hoping for a different outcome. Leveraging historical data is a way to keep you sane.

Expected ROI: You may not currently calculate ROI, so it will require extra work to think through what a potential return might look like. That said, if you go through this exercise it will produce a clear indicator for selecting a strategy. ROI takes into account your cost of execution and removes performance ambiguity to provide the clearest measurement of success. For more information, check out Chapter 10, The New Marketing ROI.

To get started on building your strategies, try using the following template to focus your thinking. After a while, it will become instinctive, and you will quickly go through these steps in your mind when validating your strategy.

Marketing Goal	Marketing Strategy
Sales growth	• Land and expand • Promotional • Competitive replacement • Sales velocity (customer acquisition) • Pricing (transparency, increase/decrease, model, etc.) • Distribution (new sales channels/partner) • Demand generation • Customer expansion (upsell/cross-sell) • Customer retention • Target audience expansion (geographic, demographic)
Brand perception	• Wedge issue • Customer evangelism • Product and services leadership • Ratings and reviews influence • Public image • Brand building • Brand refresh • Industry analyst influence • Repositioning • Customer loyalty
Awareness	• Viral • Trial • Press blitz • Rolling thunder communications • Guerrilla marketing • Content marketing strategy • Refer a friend • Big announcement • Social • Permission marketing

Below are a few more examples to help you further visualize how to think about strategies:

Strategy	Definition & Best Use Case	Compatible campaigns
Competitive replacement	**Goal:** Expand market share **Target:** The competition's customers **Best use case:** When your competitor has a large customer base and you have a better/cheaper/easier product or service **Definition:** Make a compelling argument or offer to your competitor's customers to inspire them to switch to your product or service	• Product comparison • Undercut pricing • Competitive switch offer • Rip-out • Attack
Promotional	**Goal:** Increase sales velocity **Target:** Customers/prospects/partners **Best use case:** When you need to get sales quickly and your industry uses promotions regularly **Definition:** Market an attractive offer to inspire quick, timely sales.	• Discount • Gift with purchase • BOGO • Limited time • Bundling
Customer expansion	**Goal:** Increase the lifetime value **Target:** Customers **Best use case:** When you have additional or new products or services that your customers can benefit from. Also, if your customers are large companies with multiple divisions or regions that may not have exposure to your brand. **Definition:** Target customers with relevant product or service messaging to inspire them to buy more.	• Cross-sell • Upsell • Add on services • Customer appreciation event • Cross-departmental/region

Using strategies can help you and your team focus on the best ways to achieve your marketing goals. There is a diverse range of strategies to choose from, so analyzing your key selection factors is critical. Get your whole team involved in the strategy creation process to ensure buy-in and remove complexity. Remember, when in doubt, always refer to the data. And lastly, use your strategies to drive your campaign creation.

CHAPTER 8

Redefining Marketing Campaigns

The word "campaign" is one of the most overused terms in marketing and has come to mean just about every activity marketers do. How many times do you hear people say, "Let's do an email campaign?"

First off, one email is an activity, not a campaign. Secondly, if you have something you need to communicate, you don't start with the marketing channel. Choosing the channel comes after you know what you want to accomplish and with what audience.

So why has "campaign" blossomed into this catch-all term that basically means marketers are doing some work? Blame the technology vendors. Most marketing technologies were created by engineers who did not hold marketing positions. They needed to call activities executed in their software product something, so "campaigns" became the term of choice. Now two decades worth of marketers use the word loosely, and it has resulted in a significant amount of bad marketing.

A true marketing campaign

A campaign is a message or set of messages to be communicated to a specific audience through a variety of communication channels in order to achieve a goal. When you build your campaign plan, you need to start with what you are trying to accomplish and who you want to reach. If you don't know what you want to get out of the campaign and you don't understand the audience and their needs, then it's likely your campaign will fail. Although if you don't have a goal, then what is failure?

In an effort to understand what a campaign is in familiar terms we turn to politics. No, we are not going to get political in this book, but we just want to use a presidential election as an illustration. A presidential campaign is basically one big, long, very expensive marketing campaign. Let's use the upcoming 2020 campaign as a modern example. The candidates have a goal, they both want to be president of the United States. Their target audience is the American people. There are a set of messages that they want to communicate to the American people regarding issues such as healthcare, homeland security, and jobs. They both have a campaign theme. Then they will use a variety of marketing channels to push their messages out to the American people. Those marketing channels include press, events, advertising, social media, direct mail, telemarketing, bumper stickers, billboards, word of mouth, etc. They have a clearly defined timeline of November 2020. They both have marketing budgets in the hundreds of millions to work with to get their word out (marketers imagine the damage we could all do with that budget). And lastly, they have a measurement of success, votes.

We've only included the campaign plan essentials in order to simplify the presidential campaign example above. That said, there is a lot more detail you can add to a marketing campaign plan that will organize your strategy and tactics to ensure success.

Before you start writing your campaign plan, ask yourself or your team the following five questions:

What is the goal you are trying to accomplish?

Who is the target audience?

What are the messages you would like to communicate?

What are the most effective marketing channels to communicate the messages?

How do you measure success?

If you can answer these questions first, then you can test the feasibility and determine the best approach. Once you do that, you are ready to build out your campaign plan.

Campaign Types

Campaigns are always goals-based, but larger campaigns could satisfy multiple goals. A perfect example of this is a new product or service launch. The primary goal is to sell the new product or service. But in order to do that, you must create awareness and perception so that the buyer can make a purchasing decision. For this reason, campaigns can be multifactorial and complex.

Campaigns are a combination of marketing goals, strategy, and tactics. For example:

- Goal: Lead all competitors in share of voice
- Strategy: Leadership (assess the competition and invest in overperformance)

- Campaign: Leadership (unique ideas and content that differentiates)
- Tactics: Investment in a PR agency and writers to create content and create a cadence that outpaces the competition

Below are some common campaign types:

Campaign Types

Account-Based Marketing

Awareness

Brand Launch

Competitive Replacement

Content

Customer Acquisition

Customer Advocacy

Customer Retention/Loyalty

Customer Upsell/Cross-Sell

Demand/Lead Generation

Expansion Campaign

Integrated

Lead Nurture

Lead Re-engagement

Partner

Product Launch

Promotional

Public Relations

Rebrand

Repositioning

Thought Leadership

Viral

Now, someone might ask, "Where is the trade show campaign?" A trade show is a marketing channel, a place where potential customers congregate so you can reach a large target audience with your message. Marketing channels are a critical part of campaigns, but they are not campaigns.

What about ad campaigns? Ads by themselves are of no value without thinking about the goals you are looking to accomplish, what you want to say in the ads, and where you are going to place the ads. Also, is advertising the only thing you plan to do? Or are there other vehicles that you plan to leverage after your target audience responds to the ads? If you are not thinking beyond the ad for your campaign, then you should go back to the drawing board.

Below is a list of commonly used marketing channels so you can see the difference between these and campaign types.

Channels

Analysts

Billboard, Poster, Wrap

Content

Digital Event

Direct Mail

Email

Paid Digital Ads

Physical Events (trade shows, seminars, etc.)

Podcast

Press

Print

Radio

SEM
SEO
Social
Telemarketing
TV
Voice Assistant
Webinar
Website

As you can see from the list, channels are the way to reach the target audience. A marketing channel is an empty vehicle until you put messages in it. Then you give the vehicle a destination—the target audience.

Channels are an important part of a campaign, and the process of selecting them should not be rushed. Not all channels will perform for all audiences. For example, if your audience is not internet-savvy, stay away from digital channels. If your message is long and needs explaining, don't "tweet" it. If you're targeting an audience in Los Angeles, don't run a dinner event during rush hour.

Carefully select channels based on:

> Target audience reach (Do you need to reach a wide audience or segmented?)
> The vehicle that will best house the message (content length, imagery, etc.)
> Cost per lead (What will fit into your budget?)

Once you have mapped out the key elements of your campaign, now you must execute. Execution is a challenge for marketing organizations that are distributed (which was common in 2020 and 2021) and for teams that are set-up by function. The reason for this is that everyone owns a piece of the campaign, but in many cases there is not a dedicated campaign manager to pull it all together. If you don't have a campaign manager and plan to assign responsibility to the person on the team who has the largest role, review the following elements that are part of the campaign execution process:

Timeline: For some campaigns, timing is everything (product launches, major events, market factors, etc.). Marketers need to create a timeline that includes milestones with clear responsibilities and ownership. The timeline must be visible to all team members at all times for collaboration. Too often timelines are created in PowerPoint or Excel and are only reviewed during status meetings. This usually results in surprises and missed milestones.

Team management: Large campaigns may incorporate a lot of team resources from many marketing disciplines. The most important person for campaign team management is the campaign owner (preferably a campaign manager). This person needs project management skills and has to be organized in order to keep other team members on track. During the kick-off meeting, to set a solid foundation for success, all team members should be clear on what the goals are, who the target audience is, and what you plan to communicate.

Team meeting schedule: Since there can be a number of moving parts to a campaign, holding a team meeting at least once a week is important to stay on track. The kick-off meeting should be an ideation and team buy-in session where goals, target audiences, and themes are established. It is best during this meeting to carve out team member responsibilities for campaign execution. Follow-on campaign meetings should discuss messaging, status, activities, channels, and delivery dates. The final meeting should be a review of campaign performance. Your company may run several campaigns concurrently with a number of team members participating, if not all of them. In this scenario, it would be best to appoint a campaign owner for each campaign to lead their portion of the meeting. If your campaign strategy is complex, and budget permitting, you might want to hire a dedicated campaign manager.

Task, content, and budget management: Once your goals, target audience, and theme has been established, the execution begins. Setting clear roles and responsibilities including specific task ownership is essential to keep the team focused on campaign delivery. Content versioning and approval workflow should be part of the campaign management process to ensure quality. Lastly, keep a close eye on campaign expenses to ensure you stay on budget. Have a system to track expenses as they come in and make budget status visible to the team.

The Ultimate Campaign Template

To help you think through your campaigns in their entirety, below is a comprehensive campaign template. Not all of these fields need to be filled out for every campaign you execute, but if you are running large-scale integrated campaigns, this framework should help you pull in all the important elements. To provide more detail about what should be included, the template includes our own B2B product launch example.

Campaign Name	Best Marketing Budgeting Platform on the Planet
Campaign type	Product launch
Goals	Launch budget automation functionality Create awareness for industry- leading budget management Generate new leads Accelerate existing opportunities Upsell customers Build our database
Audience	Heads of marketing, marketing operations, and marketing budget owners
Topline Message	Introducing the first AI-driven, automated budget management software for improving team efficiency and marketing spend accuracy
Supporting Messages	Make every marketing dollar count. Stretch your marketing spend. Never reconcile marketing expenses again. Set it and forget it, marketing budgeting made easy. Marketers, need to tighten the belt? This can manage your budget. Marketers: spend more time marketing and less managing your budget. Want full visibility into your marketing spend? Goodbye spreadsheets! Automate your marketing budget.

Marketing Strategies	**Leadership** The "best marketing budget management platform" message Work with industry thought leaders to communicate the message Show measurable ROI beyond what any competitor can deliver **Growth** Customer acquisition - communicate budget automation features Customer upselling - automation package
Call to Action	View our budget management blog post series (awareness) Download eBook - "How to manage your budget when money is tight" (lead generation) Register for demo to see it in action (new business lead generation) Try our budget calculator (move through the pipeline) Read a customer ROI case study (move through the pipeline)
Metrics of success	10 news articles written about the product 1,000 registrations for a public demo webinar 100 personalized demo meetings 2,000 downloads of the ebook 3,000 new contacts in the database (from webinars, demos, eBook, newsletter, budget calculator) 300 qualified new business opportunities $1M qualified new business pipeline
Campaign Duration	Tuesday, April 7th - June 30th

Content	Blog post series (4)
	Automation for budgeting product blog
	Book series blog on budgeting #1
	Book series blog on budgeting #2
	Book series blog on budgeting #3
	Press release
	Prospect email (see a demo)
	Customer email (upsell)
	Tweeter (series)
	LinkedIn posts (series)
	Website (homepage with press release banner, product page)
	Large content asset - eBook
Marketing Vehicles (channels)	Email
	Blog
	Newsletter
	Twitter
	LinkedIn
	Facebook
	Website
	Google AdWords advertising (keywords: marketing budget software)
	LinkedIn Ads
	Webinar
	Content syndication (with eBook)
Customer Marketing Activity	Email to customers about the announcement
	Demo video of new functionality for customers
	Live customer webinar
PR/AR Activity	Issue press release (PR newswire and on the company blog)
	Post any articles on the website
	Send articles to sales for follow-up
	Send the budget automation release to industry analysts
	Send to industry influencers
Nurturing Activity	Email nurturing (5) focused on educating and driving prospects through the pipeline

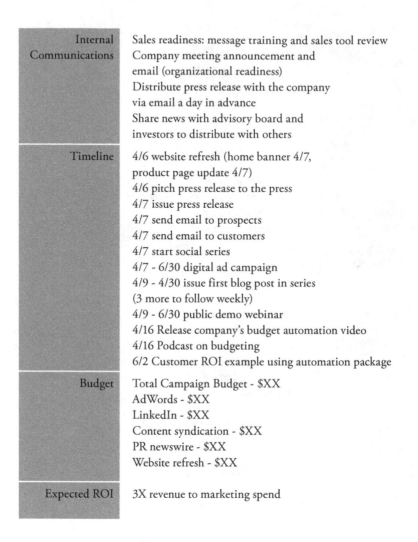

Internal Communications	Sales readiness: message training and sales tool review Company meeting announcement and email (organizational readiness) Distribute press release with the company via email a day in advance Share news with advisory board and investors to distribute with others
Timeline	4/6 website refresh (home banner 4/7, product page update 4/7) 4/6 pitch press release to the press 4/7 issue press release 4/7 send email to prospects 4/7 send email to customers 4/7 start social series 4/7 - 6/30 digital ad campaign 4/9 - 4/30 issue first blog post in series (3 more to follow weekly) 4/9 - 6/30 public demo webinar 4/16 Release company's budget automation video 4/16 Podcast on budgeting 6/2 Customer ROI example using automation package
Budget	Total Campaign Budget - $XX AdWords - $XX LinkedIn - $XX Content syndication - $XX PR newswire - $XX Website refresh - $XX
Expected ROI	3X revenue to marketing spend

Note: See appendix for a blank version of the template.

CHAPTER 9

Successful Management of Your Marketing Budget

The success of your marketing outcomes largely depends on the execution of your marketing budget. A lot of our attention tends to be focused on the execution of the programs, which is critical. In addition, though, successful marketing organizations demonstrate accurate and nimble operational management of their budgets and expenses.

Achieving mastery of the management of your budget requires:

- A common understanding throughout the marketing team of a handful of core finance principles, such as how expenses are accounted for, and what that means for when they will hit the marketing budget
- A shared understanding throughout the entire marketing team of the different categories of expense, and the life cycle of those expense categories
- A systematic approach to recapturing stranded budget, ensuring you take advantage of the Law of Small Change
- An understanding of current and future execution risk through an understanding of the Budget Burn Rate metric

- The ability to quickly run scenario analyses of budget changes and implement the preferred scenario efficiently
- The timing of insight into expenses by different company functions. For example, marketing is aware of certain expenses (e.g. credit card charges) before finance. Finance is aware of certain expenses (e.g. intra-company charges, certain accruals) before marketing

If you sustain these practices, your marketing function will benefit in numerous ways. You'll make better decisions when you have accurate, real-time visibility into what budget is available and what has been spent. You'll accurately consume your budget on time, in alignment with your marketing goals. You'll avoid over- and under-spend, over-priced rush jobs, and losing budget to use-it-or-lose-it company policies. You'll also be responsive and responsible in replanning scenarios due to external factors or company performance, and will be able to accurately measure ROI.

There is no downside to managing your budget accurately, and by implementing a fairly small number of steps, you will be able to significantly enhance the likelihood of achieving better marketing outcomes.

Five financial fundamentals that every marketer needs to understand

Even though most marketers don't get the accounting training they need, it is important that everyone responsible for significant marketing spend understands a few key accounting principles and how they apply to their marketing budgets. Five important concepts to know are: cash-based accounting, accrual-based accounting, expense recognition, roll-forward, and use-or-lose-it. Understanding these will protect you, your budget, your team, and your company from the unwanted consequences of major over- and underspend in your marketing budget.

Cash-based versus accrual-based accounting

Most articles you read about these two different types of accounting focus on revenue and expenses. However, for most marketers, the focus is primarily on expenses, so that will be our focus, too. Given that, what does it even mean to account for an expense? *Investopedia* describes accounting as, "the practice of recording financial transactions pertaining to a business." We would add a phrase to make this a bit more useful: "Accounting is the practice of recording financial transactions pertaining to a business, *in the most informative way possible.*" Accounting helps explain what has happened financially in the business, so it needs to be comprehensible and clear.

There are two high-level approaches to accounting: Cash-based accounting and accrual-based accounting:

Cash-based accounting

Cash-based accounting records expenses when they are paid. This is normally not the most informative method of accounting.

In cash-based accounting, the relevant expense hits the financial books at the time the funds leave the company bank account. In some ways this seems intuitive. It is how most of us are used to managing our personal finances. But for most companies, it's not particularly useful.

There is often a period of time between the cash outlay and the activity that generated the cash outlay. And this approach builds that difference right into the company's books. If accounting is supposed to tell the story of the business, this approach obscures the real story. The date a bill happens to be paid is hard to predict, so cash-based accounting creates a narrowly accurate, but somewhat arbitrary, record of the business.

While a business may well want to *pay* for something six months after they received it, it doesn't want to *account* for it that late. It's just too difficult to keep track of what that expense was for, when you consider the large number of diverse expenses the business incurs over time.

Additionally, the gold standards for business accounting - Generally Accepted Accounting Principles (GAAP) and International Financial Reporting Standards (IFRS) - do not support cash-based accounting, and most companies don't want to report their accounts in non-standard ways.

Accrual-based accounting

Accrual-based accounting uses the notion of *value* to account for expenses. This method is required for GAAP and IFRS accounting. In accrual-based accounting, marketing costs may be recorded differently depending on what they are. Certain costs, like printing jobs, will normally be recognized upon invoice. On the other hand, recognition of event expenses will often be deferred until the date of the event, and all recognized on the same day as the event.

Why does it make sense to recognize expenses on different dates? The idea is to make the state of the business clearer to observers such as executives, investors, and auditors. By aligning expense recognition of event costs with the date of the expense itself, it is easier to discern how much the event cost. If all the expenses in the run up to the event were recognized as they came in, it would be almost impossible to discern from an accounting system what the event actually cost.

So, in accrual-based accounting, there is an association and a matching between *when an expense is recognized* in the company accounts, and *when the company receives value*. Finance teams try to adopt a consistent approach about when the various types of expenses are recognized for their company, but companies have some latitude about how they operate as long as they are consistent.

As marketers move from company to company throughout their careers, they need to understand how each new company does things. It's important for marketers to understand the timing of expense recognition within their company so that they can plan accurately.

Here is an example:

Company X wants to run an ad campaign on TV. It outsources 100% of the ad production costs ($500,000) to AdAgencyCo. Company X also purchases a $1,000,000 media buy on a TV station. Company X receives the invoices for the ad production and the media buy on the same day. That date happens to be after the production is complete, but two months before the ads will air on TV. The $500,000 production costs are recognized when the invoices are received, because the value received by the company is the finished ad. So, the bills for the ad production must be recognized when production is completed, regardless of when (or whether) the ad airs. The $1,000,000 media buy is recognized in the books two months later, when the ad is aired.

It is important for the marketers at Company X to understand when the costs for their campaign will be recognized, otherwise they might find expenses hitting their budget in unexpected time frames. (Note: this is not the *only* way the investment can be accounted for in an accruals-based approach, but it is one valid method that is provided as an example in GAAP guidance to help illuminate time-based recognition of different marketing costs).

Sometimes an accounting team might accrue an expense before an invoice is even received. It might do this if there is a highly predictable billing cycle and well-established value for a given bill. For example, many companies have contracts with SaaS companies that invoice on a monthly basis. The SaaS contract may call for payment of $1,000 on the first of every month. Accounting may well decide to accrue the $1,000 expense even if the invoice hasn't arrived by the first of a given month. This makes sense, because there's a legally binding contract in place that stipulates a $1,000 expense every month. If nobody canceled the service, there's surely a bill coming; it's common sense to account for it.

This method of accounting makes business finances more readable, traceable, and understandable for everyone, because it shows expenses as being accounted for in the same time period as the value received. That matching principle is a cornerstone of good accounting.

The Impact on Marketing Budgets

This matters a lot to marketers. Your marketing budget is distributed over time, probably months or quarters. There is some allocation of funds in the plan that assumes you will spend the budget at a certain rate each time period. Your goal is to spend it down to the last penny (but no more) and to spend it on the most goal-aligned activities you possibly can. If you don't know how your expenses are being accounted for, then you don't know what you've spent for a given time period's budget. Look at this treatment of the same expense under cash-based versus accrual-based accounting:

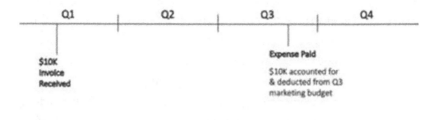

**Cash-based accounting separates value
impact from budget impact**

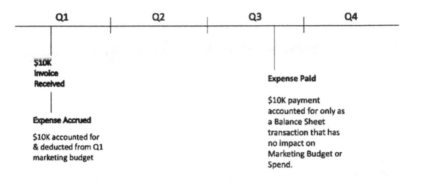

Accrual-based accounting aligns value impact with budget impact

In cash-based accounting, the expense was deducted from the Q3 budget. In accrual-based accounting, it was deducted from the Q1 budget. For most marketers, the accrual-based system makes much more sense—their expenses are accounted for when they are invoiced. This is much easier to plan for in order to manage spending accurately. As a marketer, you should not need to care when the cash has left the company bank account, or what the CFO is doing on the balance sheet.

Expense Recognition in Accrual-Based Accounting

There is one other critical element of accrual-based accounting that is important to familiarize yourself with: when are expenses recognized? Didn't we just say they're recognized upon invoice? Not quite. We said they're accounted for upon recognition of *value*. It is possible that you might be invoiced for a service, may even *pay* for a service, before it delivers business value. The most common marketing example of such an instance is an events

Consider the diagram below, where marketing incurs multiple expenses prior to, during, and even shortly after, a trade show:

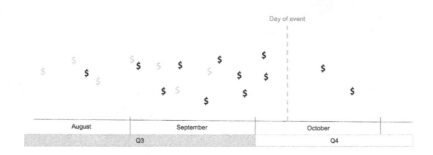

Expenses for a major event occur over a long time period

The gray expenses represent those that have been invoiced and paid. The black expenses represent expenses that have not yet been invoiced and/or paid. Under accrual-based accounting, it is possible that 100% of these expenses will be recognized by the company on the day of the event because this is when the company received value for all of the expenses related to the event. From an accounting perspective, that looks like this:

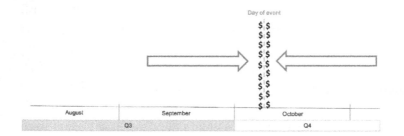

**Accrual of diverse expenses, with a
simultaneous budget impact**

Suddenly, we see expenses appearing in what might feel like the wrong quarter again, even under accrual-based accounting. Confusingly, expenses that the marketer *knows* have been paid may be moved in the company accounts to align with the event date (when the value was received). In the finance report of expenses, this will normally show as a negative value (e.g., -$50,000) in the time period where the expense was originally paid and a new, equivalent positive value on the date of the event. Nothing has really changed other than the date the company has decided to account for the expense, but you need to know whether and how that impacts your marketing budget—preferably when you create your plan.

It's important that the marketing team knows when accrued expenses will be recognized so that they know how to budget accurately at the beginning of the year and when expenses will be deducted from the budget, no matter when the invoices land.

At a minimum, marketers should be sure to understand how expenses for campaign types that trigger deferred expense recognition (like trade shows) are treated by finance. Failing to do so could lead to significant underspend in certain quarters (because you thought you were accruing event expenses but you weren't) and significant overspend in others (because all the expenses for an event hit at once, and you thought you'd already paid for them).

Understanding expense treatment for your budget is not just a CMO responsibility. All marketers running campaigns (especially events) and spending the company's money need to have a keen sense of how their investments are accounted for.

Roll-Forward versus Use-it-or-Lose-It

Some companies set a budget for the year, and if not all of the anticipated Q1 budget is spent, the difference is rolled forward into Q2, and so on, through the year.

Others operate on what is known as a use-it-or-lose-it basis. If you fall into this camp, the need to understand how expenses are accounted for is even keener. Under use-it-or-lose-it budgets, there are normally soft boundaries between months (unused budget from

January can be rolled into February) but hard boundaries between quarters (unused Q1 funds are taken back by the company, and the Q2 budget remains unchanged).

Returning to our event example, imagine the total cost of that trade show was $250K. The marketing team anticipated that $150K would come from the Q3 budget and $100K would come from the Q4 budget.

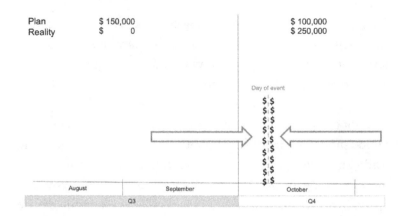

The impact of planning without accounting alignment

Unfortunately, the entire $250K came from Q4. Under a use-it-or-lose-it policy, the $150K underspend in Q3 is taken back by the company, and the Q4 budget has an unexpected additional $150K of closed expenses to fund. That means Q4 needs to be radically replanned at very short notice or the budget will be badly over-spent.

The Law of Small Change

When Dan was growing up, his father used to save for family vacations by putting the small change he had in his pocket into a large glass jar at the end of the day. When the jar was full, the family would empty it out to sort and count the coins and tally up its contents.

Every year the family was absolutely floored by how large the total was. How could these tiny, borderline worthless, increments add up to something as meaningful as a *vacation*? Every year it worked. And it *felt* like a free holiday. But of course, it wasn't free - it was enabled by what we call the Law of Small Change (LSC).

The key to the LSC working was the discipline Dan's dad had about the process. Every day, without fail, when he got home from work, he'd retrieve whatever coins were in his pocket and drop them into the jar. If he'd only done it occasionally, the jar's contents would never have amounted to anything. If he'd left the coins on a side table from time to time instead of putting them in the jar, the same amount of money would have been in the house, but the vacation fund wouldn't grow enough, and the family probably wouldn't have done anything with it. It was the consistency, the repetition, and the routine that made it happen.

This concept is relevant to marketing budgets. Marketing teams accrue piles of small change at amazing velocity and in diverse ways. There's no other function in which so many people are empowered to spend so much and so frequently.

We're going to highlight nine key ways in which marketing leaves small (and sometimes not so small) amounts of cash stranded in the nooks and crannies of its marketing budget. We'll also highlight how these piles add up to shockingly large totals. But as a preview, **most marketing budgets are losing 0.8 - 2.1% of their budget to subtle forms of waste accumulated from numerous small issues.** Since percentages seem small, here's what that could mean in real money:

Budget Size	0.8% of budget	2.1% of budget
$1,000,000	$8,000	$21,000
$2,000,000	$16,000	$42,000
$4,000,000	$32,000	$84,000
$10,000,000	$80,000	$210,000
$25,000,000	$200,000	$525,000

One thing to be clear about: these losses are not due to negligence or incompetence. Rather, they're the inevitable outcome of legacy tools and platforms that are unfit to manage complex marketing budgets that change a lot.

Here are nine key ways that marketing loses money in the marketing budget. We know these are both real and significant because we onboard and manage hundreds of real marketing budgets, and our marketing database shows us the facts.

1. Not reviewing the marketing budget regularly

A marketing team should spend every last cent of its budget in the most thoughtful way possible, and not a penny more. Marketing teams that don't regularly review the status of their budgets and maintain a current view of the state of the budget don't have a chance of doing this. Most months, they will overspend or underspend, culminating in a major miss by the end of the year.

One of our customers reported that before using our platform, her team reached the end of the fiscal year to be told by finance that they had underspent by tens of thousands of dollars on a budget of less than $1,000,000. That money could have delivered meaningful business results. The VP of Marketing didn't know, because they didn't have a process and platform that supported a current view of the marketing ins and outs.

2. Not reviewing the budget as a team

We requested a customer bring their entire marketing team to a training session. During the meeting, as we reviewed their budget, a budget owner piped up, "This is awesome. I didn't even realize I **had** a $50,000 budget in Q2."

Why didn't that person know? This was a smart team run by a strong VP of Marketing. There were a few reasons, but the main one was that they did not review the budget as a whole team. There were people with buying power and budget responsibility who didn't know what they were empowered to spend and when.

3. Budget spread over multiple worksheets

A customer walked us through their budget spreadsheet prior to onboarding with us. It looked like a work of art. Beautifully laid out. Formulas pulling data from other worksheets. A separate worksheet for each budget owner, entering their data into a common template. The problem was, the totals on the individual worksheets didn't match the totals on the summary worksheet. And the totals on the individual worksheets didn't add up to the full budget target.

It required forensic analysis and some black-belt spreadsheet skills to figure out all the errors. The problem is, spreadsheets fail silently. If someone hard codes a number on top of a formula in one cell, enters a number as text in another, inserts a row that's not included in a formula in another, multiple little piles of wasted budget are distributed throughout the complex spreadsheet, hidden in plain sight. Every incremental worksheet or spreadsheet, and every incremental user working in the spreadsheet, increases the frequency and likelihood of errors.

4. Poor visibility into the budget

One budget we onboarded had run out of funds for two of its four divisions at the end of the eighth month of the fiscal year. Every penny in the last third of the year was 100% over budget. The budget owner didn't know this because his spreadsheet, provided by finance, was so complex that it was genuinely difficult to understand what was contained within it.

5. Stranded budget in completed campaigns and closed expenses

One company realized that it had 23% of its budget still available to spend, and they had only two weeks left in their budget year to spend it—an impossible task. That 23% was an accumulation of numerous small differences between planned and actual expenses, and small underspends in completed campaigns, that had accrued throughout the year. Just like the vacation money jar, they added up to a significant total. They could have added tremendous business value if they'd been easily visible to everyone on the team.

6. Inaccurate budget tracking lost to a use-it-or-lose policy

One of our customers routinely lost between 5% and 10% of her budget each year because it was difficult to spend her budget in time with the existing budget tools. This customer didn't have a current view of what had been spent, so she was nervous to overspend as she approached the end of the quarter. Once the expenses were reconciled, any remaining budget was lost for good.

7. Overpaying due to multiple rush orders

Rush charges occur (most of the time, at least) when a poorly planned expense is incurred. "Poorly planned" means the team finds itself making an investment in something services-based without leaving time to negotiate a fair price. Common examples of this are printing, design and booth needs for events. Typically, the marketing team will find itself overpaying by at least 10% for such expenses.

8. Not reconciling expenses with finance

One prospect who did *not* become a customer (you'll see why in a minute) was a CMO who told us that he did not reconcile any expenses in his multi-million-dollar annual budget. We expressed surprise that this was so, since he acknowledged he had no way of knowing his current expenditure with any accuracy. His outlier status was confirmed when he stated that he was okay as long as the budget was "within about 20% of the target by the end of the year." If your company is okay with your budget being 20% inaccurate, then careful budget management is clearly not a priority.

If your company is not okay with that, then you need to reconcile your expenses—and just committing to reconciling them is not enough. You need to understand what you have spent as soon as possible. Unfortunately, turnaround time for expense reconciliation is painfully slow. This creates lots of small piles of stranded budget throughout the plan, which are difficult to track, and add to the cumulative budget risk.

9. Making mistakes in expense reconciliation

One of our customers generated a 19% budget inaccuracy by adding up the planned and actual expenses—all thanks to a spreadsheet design error. While this is a gross error, there are numerous manual reconciliation errors that occur over the course of a year such as failing to close expenses, closing them for the wrong amount, accepting expenses from other departments, logging expenses in the incorrect currency, and so on. Every one of these errors leaves a small pile of wasted budget.

Our database shows us that companies consistently generate cumulative budget risks of 15%-25% annually due to an aggregation of the issues above, over the course of the fiscal year. In other words, they lose 0.8% - 2.1% of their budget each month to the Law of Small Change. There is a tremendous opportunity to reclaim that lost budget—the marketing equivalent of a free vacation. After all, who wouldn't like a 15-25% budget increase?

Budget Burn Rate

We know that responsible marketing teams should not overspend. It causes P&L issues, can disrupt the marketing cadence if campaigns have to be canceled because the budget has been exhausted, and leads to general disharmony. Something that receives less attention, but is equally important, is marketing underspend.

One of our favorite customers came to us because his finance team had told him that marketing was underspending chronically throughout the fiscal year. The problem was opaque to him because of the existing tools and processes—the typical combination of spreadsheet-based marketing budget and episodic accounting system dumps from finance. It was impossible to have real-time visibility into what had been spent and what was left in the budget for that time period.

As the team moved through the year, they didn't know whether they could make that next significant purchase, or whether that would take them over budget, so they did what most responsible corporate citizens did: nothing. Better to be under budget and safe than potentially over budget, right? And they could always roll forward any unspent budget into the next time period and spend it then.

Unfortunately, this is not the right way to manage your marketing budget. You can't endlessly roll forward unspent funds because the end of the fiscal year (or fiscal quarter) is a brick wall. At some point you find yourself up against the wall, and the unspent funds piled up against it are swept into the corporate coffers, having added no value to the business.

That might mean the company saves a little money, but it also means the marketing team has demonstrated that it does not have the wherewithal to spend the budget it was allocated. Worse, they have not delivered the business benefits of the marketing investments they failed to make. This can raise questions about whether marketing is operationally sound. Since actual spending typically sets the baseline for the next year's budget, underspend can lead to year-over-year reductions in marketing budget.

The Underspend Conundrum

It is probably worth bringing to the fore a critical, but implicit point: marketing needs to spend 100% of its budget, spend it promptly, and spend it thoughtfully. If this seems obvious, it isn't to many marketers and corporate cultures that think it is a virtue to come in under budget. It is not. It's a virtue to spend less on electricity than you intended, or to implement a corporate IT project under budget. But marketing underspend fails the business and can lead to unwanted consequences, as illustrated below.

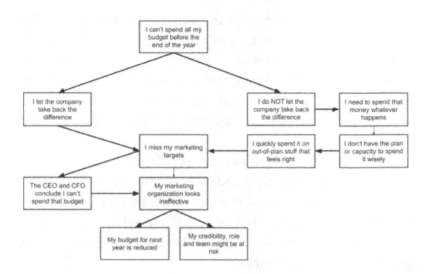

The Underspend Conundrum leads to numerous problems

If marketing underspends, then it breaks its agreement with the company about what it is going to deliver in terms of pipeline, leads, brand enhancements, awareness and so on. In an ideal world, a marketing team spends every penny of its budget aligned with marketing goals and against a well-structured plan.

With the existing systems in place for managing marketing budgets at most companies, this is impossible. Not *nearly* impossible. It's impossible in every practical sense. Most marketers discover what they have spent somewhere between six and eight weeks after the fact. This time lag necessarily crosses monthly budget boundaries, and frequently runs into harder quarterly budget boundaries. If you don't have visibility into what budget is available right now, and you know that heads will roll if you overspend, it is human nature to slow down in moments of uncertainty. If those moments of uncertainty are frequent enough, you will have the same kind of chronic underspend that our customer was experiencing.

The first step is to do what that customer did and move your plan and budget onto software that provides real-time visibility into planned, committed and invoiced expenditures. You don't have to wait for the final payments to be made by finance, and then to receive the accounts payable or open PO report to have that current visibility. You just need a system to track it. You can always interlock to the penny with the finance system once their reports land in your inbox, but there is no need to fly blind in the meantime.

Another key step you can take is to get familiar with the concept of Budget Burn Rate (BBR).

Let's make and test a key assertion: when a marketing leader finalizes his or her marketing plan and budget, he or she will have in place a staffing and resource capacity (or at least a capacity plan) to execute the plan and spend the budget within the fiscal year. Are there enough full-time employees, contractors, consultants, agencies, tools, etc., in place to actually deliver the plan that's on paper? Our assertion is that the majority of the time, the CMO has verified this, and believes that the plan and budget is efficiently executable with the resources on hand.

This assumption is critically important to the concept of BBR. Most CMOs have some degree of interlock between their marketing budget and their capacity to spend that budget in a thoughtful way. We only care about this assertion in the abstract for now. While it's true that a small team doing nothing but digital campaigns can burn through a huge budget quickly compared to a team that does nothing but field marketing and regional events, we believe that the capacity of a marketing team (not just FTEs, but all contract labor and agencies as well) is normally at least roughly right-sized to the nature of the marketing plan, its required campaigns and tactics, and the size of the budget to support it.

Budget Burn Rate (BBR) is a function of change, like miles per hour, gross domestic product per capita, calories per slice of pizza, etc. In the case of BBR, we are measuring how much budget needs to be spent per time period for the remainder of the year in order to consume 100% of the budget accurately and in alignment with the marketing plan. We've picked a day as the unit of time. It could be a week or a month, but the bigger the time unit, the less granularity we have.

Imagine you have a budget of $1,800,000 for a fiscal year. Regardless of how you intend to allocate the budget over time and by campaign, you need to consume that budget in the next 365 days. On day 1 of your fiscal year, your required average BBR is $1,800,000/365 = $4,932/day. Now let's assume that you decide to allocate your budget across the months like this:

Budget	**$ 1,800,000**
January	$ 100,000
February	$ 120,000
March	$ 150,000
April	$ 140,000
May	$ 145,000
June	$ 170,000
July	$ 190,000
August	$ 130,000
September	$ 145,000
October	$ 160,000
November	$ 160,000
December	$ 190,000

It doesn't matter that the allocations by month are different from each other, nor that the most expensive months require the team to consume 190% of the least expensive month's budget. We assume that there is a marketing capacity in place that is right-sized to consume this budget at this rate over the course of the entire year.

After January, there are 334 days left, and if the entire $100K that was budgeted for January has been spent, the required BBR for the remainder of the year is now ($1,800,000 - $100,000)/334 = $5,090/day. If the budget is spent perfectly, here's what the curve for the daily BBR looks like over the course of the year:

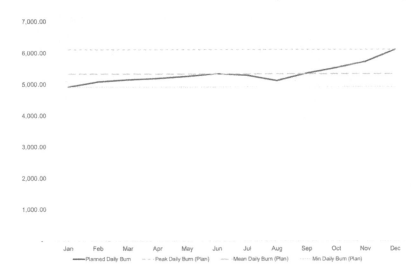

Planned BBR with Minimum, Mean and Maximum lines

The dotted line indicates the minimum daily burn rate, the thick dashed line shows the mean daily burn rate, and the dashed line at the top shows the maximum daily burn rate required to consume the budget on-time, with a range of $4,932 - $6,129/day. As long as the burn rate stays within those bounds, the capacity of the team should be well sized to execute the marketing plan and fully consume the budget on time.

Now, let's say that as the year gets underway, the team consistently spends a little *less* than planned each month. For this example, we also assume that any underspend is continuously rolled forward month-to-month.

Traditionally, this kind of delta would normally be portrayed using something like the chart below. In this chart, the solid gray line indicates the original plan, the black line indicates the cumulative actuals and the gray dotted line indicates the cumulative underspend. It doesn't look *that* bad.

At first blush, it looks like the team tracked along roughly accurately but finished the overall plan fairly close to the original. In reality, this is a 10.5% underspend—that's a large discrepancy from the original plan. That most likely means that there are significant shortfalls in pipeline, bookings, leads, impressions, and so on that the business now needs to cope with.

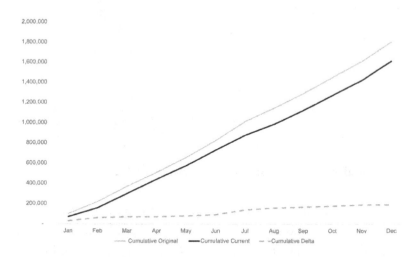

Typical comparison of planned vs. actual budget usage

This is also not a particularly helpful view analytically because it isn't actionable. If we cast this same data onto a BBR view, however, we see something more alarming, more realistic, and more actionable:

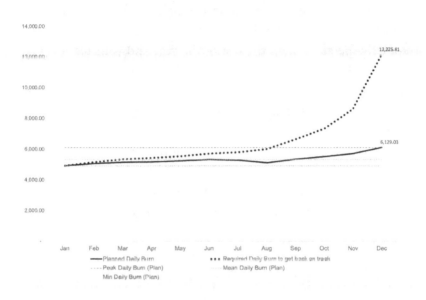

BBR representation of planned vs. actual, indicating growing execution risk over time

As the underspend accumulates over the year, we can see the required daily BBR (the thick dotted line) begins to increase and separates from the planned daily BBR (the solid line). In early August, the required BBR breaks through the maximum BBR for the year (remember, that approximates the maximum capacity of the team).

As the underspend piles up month to month, the required BBR accelerates away from the planned BBR. This is because the time available to spend the rolled forward budget is running out—there's more money to spend than we thought there would be in a shrinking time frame. We're about to hit the end-of-year wall.

Imagine you are the CMO running this budget and it's November. You have a lot of money to spend. Your team is fully occupied executing as much of the plan as they can, but they've been consistently under-spending throughout the year. What are you going to do? You need to spend twice as much money as you normally spend through the rest of the year and your team is fully occupied. Look back again at the Underspend Conundrum flow chart above and you will see there are not many good choices. Marketing teams find themselves in this position all the time.

Do you need to careen into the year-end wall, frantically trying to spend more money than you can, knowing you're not spending it wisely?

We believe BBR can help avoid these situations. As soon as we see the BBR begin to deviate above the plan BBR, we know we're underspending.

As the gap begins to widen, the risk increases. Before it approaches your maximum team capacity, you need to begin to increase your BBR so that you can pull the actual BBR line back in order to match the planned BBR line. Perhaps you need to hire some more temp help, or open the throttle on that digital campaign. The remediation is case dependent, but the value of bringing the current and plan BBR into alignment is clear—it means you can finish the year spending your money intentionally, phased appropriately over time, and in accordance with your strategic goals. If you'd been measuring BBR, you would have seen this move of the actual BBR line towards your maximum capacity early in the year and would have been able to take action while still in the first half of the year.

Accurate expense management

An expense is an expense, right? In the sense that they all hit your budget, yes. In most other respects, not really. The team dinner check, the hotel block booking for a trade show, the rush print job for the key customer visit, the dreaded expense that's transferred in from another department, the CRM subscription—these are different types of expenses that have very different life cycles. Some of them you can, and should, plan for. Some you need to know will happen anyway and accommodate in your planning.

There's a pretty finite set of expense types that you will have to deal with. In this section, we're first going to deal with the life cycle of a typical expense, and then we'll talk about how different expense categories fit within (or occasionally violate) this life cycle. Once you know this, you will be able to look at the expenses in your plan and budget with fresh eyes, to make sure you're treating them in the way that's most useful to you and your team.

The Expense Life Cycle

An expense is first estimated, then committed, charged, and reconciled. Let's look at these steps in more detail:

Estimated: You have to estimate expenses all the time. You know you're going to need to book some rooms and pay for some meals at that upcoming event, or hire a creative agency for that upcoming campaign. When you know about these expenses in advance, you should estimate what the expenses will be. Planned expenses should have estimated amounts.

Committed: Some expenses will be large enough and far enough in the future that you decide to negotiate the price with a vendor. You may sign a contract to lock in that price along with other terms. You might sign up a PR agency for a campaign, a creative agency to help you prepare for an event, or a new technology platform to automate some of your marketing processes. Once you've signed the contract, you have a more precise view of the cost than your initial estimate, and you know you're really on the hook to pay that money. You haven't been invoiced, the service hasn't been delivered, but you know you're going to be paying a precise amount in the future. Negotiated expenses should have very accurate cost estimates.

Charged: Expenses are charged, from the marketer's perspective, once the service has been delivered, or once an invoice has been sent. The expense should be marked as charged regardless of whether or not it has been *paid* by finance. What the marketing team should care about first and foremost is how much budget has been consumed and how much is left. Surprisingly frequently, we have met marketers who are concerned about when and whether a bill has been paid. It's important to understand when a bill is charged against your budget, but when a bill is *paid* is a finance team concern that does not affect how much marketing budget is left. Our recommendation is that you treat invoicing as the trigger to mark an expense as charged. Likewise, you should treat credit card expenses as charged.

Reconciled: The majority of marketing teams receive a periodic report from finance that includes the accounting system view of all the paid bills that have been charged to marketing. Most of the time this will contain line-by-line confirmations of what you already know and have in your plan. However, the final accounting of expenses may well contain changes that you need to know about and pay attention to. For example, you didn't anticipate the sales tax for your finally negotiated price, and the cost that finance has to account for is a little higher than you thought. Or, finance has charged something to marketing that is a surprise to you and wasn't in your plan. This could include some credit card expense that you didn't know existed, an expense transferred in from another department, or a change of date to an expense due to accruals-based accounting.

In any case, it's imperative that you snap your plan into line with the finance team's report to ensure that your pretty-darn-accurate view of the charged marketing expenses ultimately aligns with the financial system of record. The problem is, you can't wait weeks or months for those finance reports or you're flying blind, and it's impossible to spend accurately, decisively, and at the right budget burn rate. So, you need to develop and manage a *highly* accurate team-sourced view of the reality of your charged expenses, well ahead of the finance report. Demanding accurate, real-time expense status from the entire marketing team will enable you to make fact-based, accurate decisions on time.

Accuracy at different expense life cycle stages

Now that you understand the stages, let's review the different types of expenses and how to manage them to best achieve your marketing goals.

Carried-over expenses

When you enter your budget year, your budget should contain a number of expenses that are estimated, committed and possibly even charged and reconciled. You should try to get those into your plan in as much detail as possible, so you have an accurate forecast of spend and a clear understanding of what's left to spend. Examples of these include: campaigns that cross fiscal year boundaries, events that you do every year, subscription fees for data or technology, open POs for contractors or agencies, corporate allocations, and depreciation. Many of these expenses will be at least charged, and often reconciled, on day 1 of the fiscal year.

Planned expenses

Planned expenses are the way it happens in marketing textbooks, and sometimes this is the way it happens in reality.

If you have a new campaign, set of expenses, or an individual expense that you know is new for the fiscal year, you should enter it into your plan with the most accurate estimate of the expense that you can manage. It doesn't matter if it's imperfect—it's much better to have something in your budget than nothing.

Examples include event expenses that are known in advance (block room booking, travel, meals, booth expenses, printing, agencies, etc.), a digital campaign with an estimated spend-per-day ceiling, technology and data subscriptions, contractor retainers, and so on. There are *many* unplanned expenses that will crop up through the year, so the more thoroughly you can add your planned expenses into your budget, the better you will have visibility into what remains to be spent, and how close to over budget you are.

Planned expenses may be large enough that you have to raise a PO and negotiate price and payment terms, or they may be small, or fast-moving enough that they are charged to a credit card without a PO or contract.

You may plan an aggregate cost for a group of expenses and reserve budget for them. We call this an "expense bucket." In this context, we use expense buckets to estimate the cost of a set of expenses for which it may not be possible (or a good use of time) to estimate the line-by-line costs for each individual expense.

For example, you might budget an amount for travel every month even though you don't know the precise make-up of taxi rides, train fares, air fares and car mileage that is going to come in. Such expenses will likely be charged to credit cards, maybe even paid by cash, and won't be explicitly in the marketing plan with line-byline precision. When you first see them as individual expenses, they will already be committed, or even reconciled, and they should be charged to the marketing budget you reserved for them as they come in.

Unanticipated expenses

No one likes unanticipated expenses, but they happen all the time. We normally become aware of these expenses when we receive our finance report. What's unpleasant about these costs is that they are not planned and often already charged and accounted for the first time you see them.

It makes a lot of sense to try to understand your surprise expense run-rate if you can. If you don't know what it is, look at some historical data and try to find expenses like this: accounting reclassifications (an expense is moved in to your budget from another department), a corporate allocation you didn't know about, or someone misused the corporate credit card and you have to eat the cost.

You may also encounter surprise expenses from unforeseen issues. You may have unexpected PR costs from a crisis management project such as customer, press, investor and analyst communications after a data breach. Or you may have to make a major mid-year adjustment in your plan due to some major external factor, like a natural disaster.

Disputed expenses

When you get a surprise expense, you may conclude it doesn't really belong in your budget. This is a very common occurrence, and it pays to be diligent. You have enough to worry about without paying another department's bills.

Corporate and departmental allocations are frequent candidates to be disputed. You need to track the expense in your budget as if it's going to be paid by you until finance agrees to move it.

Moving expenses

You planned it. You know what date the invoice arrived and how much it was for. You know it belongs to marketing. So why can't you find it in the expense report?

As we've discussed earlier, it's important to understand how your finance team accounts for expenses. Otherwise, you may find that expenses you thought hit your budget in one time period actually were applied in a different one. This can lead to inadvertent underspend or overspend, even if you've been diligently tracking your expenses prior to interlocking with the finance team.

Timing of insight into expenses by function

There is an imperfect alignment between the finance view and the marketing view of expenses at almost every stage of the fiscal year. If expense reconciliation is taking place on a regular basis, there should be a common understanding of all expenses that have been accounted for between the beginning of the fiscal year to the end of the last period for which the accounting books were closed. But that doesn't cover everything.

There are likely to be other misalignments. For example, marketing always knows about expenses that finance does not yet know about. Increasingly, these are credit card charges that marketing has taken, but for which finance has not yet received that month's credit card invoice.

Likewise, unreported cash expenses consume marketing budget before finance is aware that they exist. It is important for the marketing team to keep track of these expenses as accurately as possible in addition to the most current accounting view of marketing expenses.

Similarly, there will always be accounting activities that don't relate to clearly identifiable marketing expenses. Purchase orders

(POs) are one such example. A PO is essentially permission to spend a certain amount on a specific thing or vendor. The funds approved in a PO are consumed by invoices charged against it.

A finance team may make certain assumptions about when POs will really be recognized as expenses. In some respect, they have to. If they accrue expenses in a way that is misaligned with what's really happening, there will be a delta between the finance assumption of accrued expenses and the marketing view of actuals. In a use-it-or-lose-it model this can have real consequences. But even outside those models, it can cause serious misalignment and confusion. It's a good practice to make sure that someone in marketing tracks what expenses have really been charged against all open POs, and whether any open POs should be closed without consuming 100% of the PO-approved amounts. Communicating this with the finance team will ensure a better common understanding of what's really been spent in marketing at any given moment.

Other examples of finance actions that may affect the marketing budget, and which might be easy for marketing to miss, include intra-company charges and incorrect accrual assumptions (e.g., assuming a subscription should be booked as a one-time expense). Due to all these opportunities for confusion, there is clearly mutual benefit in maintaining strong relationships between marketing and finance.

A note on credit card expenses

The section above on the timing of insight into expenses is particularly important in relation to credit card spending. In recent years, the percentage of marketing spend that hits credit cards has exploded. Many corporate card programs support the notion of purchasing cards (p-cards) and pre-approved virtual cards. These models allow marketing teams to spend with greater autonomy and control. However, they do not lend themselves to creating great shared visibility with finance.

If you look at the accounting report for most companies, there is a single line item that references the entire invoiced amount on the credit card bill, with no line item details. This makes it almost impossible for a marketer to reconcile with their history of marketing expenses. And, as we have highlighted, when marketers are uncertain about their budget commitments, they underspend and fail to achieve their goals.

Therefore, it's important for a marketing team to accurately track 100% of its credit card expenses. That way they can maintain a strong interlock with the finance report, and they can maintain visibility into credit card charges that finance is currently unaware of, giving them the most accurate view of marketing spend at all times.

The Unified Expense Model

The following figure is the Unified Expense Model. It shows when, during the different points throughout the expense life cycle, that different types of expenses may be initiated, the evidence for their existence, and the phases they will occupy until they are reconciled. It's possible that your expenses won't work exactly like this. That will depend on the specific policies and practices adopted by your company.

It is important that you and your marketing team understand how expenses are handled in your company's marketing budget. If you understand this well, you will be able to both plan and execute your spending with a high degree of accuracy to achieve your marketing goals.

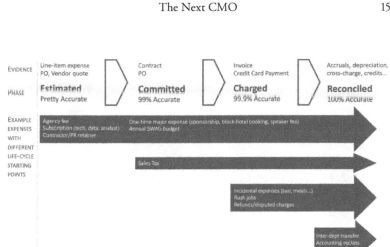

The Unified Expense Model

CHAPTER 10

The New Marketing ROI

To measure ROI, you must have a consistent and realistic measure of return, and the only consistent and real measurements of return are financial targets. Therefore, you must begin by stating your desired financial targets.

You should also be able to state up front what your desired ROI is. Too frequently, marketers carry out activities and then wonder what those activities were worth. This is backwards—marketers should define their target ROI at the outset.

If you know your financial targets and your ROI targets, it is simple to calculate your target marketing budget. Campaigns should then be devised to meet the financial target with the appropriately-sized budget.

This is not the typical approach to calculating Marketing ROI (MROI), to the detriment of the function. Marketers tend to measure what they can rather than what they should. Therefore, they tend to report on second-order metrics (impressions, views, likes, downloads, attendees) that are difficult to square with financial value. They also tend to measure at the wrong granularity.

Ultimately what matters in marketing is whether the marketing efforts are generating financial value to the company. Any metric that is decoupled from financial value has an undesirable level of indirection. This is not to say that all metrics must be financial, but they must all be demonstrably connected to a measurable financial outcome.

The more ROI can be grounded in financial targets, the better the team can communicate the value of marketing within and outside the team, the more credibility it will have in justifying its budget requests and explaining its results, and the easier it is to communicate the impacts of budget changes. This is achievable, but it may require looking at the deceptively simple ROI calculation in a new way.

The high-level challenge of measuring MROI

Marketing ROI (MROI) is known to be difficult to measure. The concept is simple. Indeed, the formula is just a twist on a standard ROI calculation:

$$\text{MROI} = (\text{Business value from Marketing - Marketing Investment})/\text{Marketing Investment}$$

The challenge that most marketers encounter is in consistently defining and capturing the data needed to fill in the variables in the equation. Let's start with the easier of the two variables: Marketing Investment. What should that include?

Let's imagine a digital campaign—should you include the media buy? It seems pretty clear you should. What about the creative agency you used to make the content for that specific campaign? Yes. How about a prorated share of the content writer you have on retainer? She contributed to it, after all, but how much time was it exactly, and what were her rates again? What about a prorated share of the company FTEs? Corporate overhead? Meals for the meetings you had with the agency? A share of the SEO optimization platform costs? It's tough to know precisely where to draw the line, but you can see that each of these costs changes the denominator and that's going to change the ROI.

The other key variable in the numerator is Business Value from Marketing. Revenue seems like a clear indicator of business value. But is that one-time revenue or customer lifetime value (LTV) that you should care about? How about gross margin? Bookings value is good too, but you'll need to map that to revenue formulaically. Pipeline? Opportunities? Impressions? Brand perception? Each step further up the marketing funnel, the more intangible a discrete measurement of marketing value becomes. Yet, we all know we have to carry out these activities high up the marketing funnel in order to influence the revenue that is realized at the end. Marketers want to provide data to quantify their impact, but they have to acknowledge that there's a large sensitivity in their results that will yield a broad range of potential outcomes—and that data doesn't hold up well under scrutiny from peers outside the marketing team.

Add to this core challenge the further complexities introduced by trying to measure traditional and digital channels consistently, tracing multi-channel campaigns, and attempting to compare your performance to industry peers, and the challenges just multiply.

Historical context of Marketing ROI

Here's a quote from a recent article about shifts in marketing investment, published on the website *Search Engine Land* (our bold):

> "While marketers should ideally address the full funnel, most no longer have the budget. Accordingly, they're emphasizing performance campaigns **because those are easier to track.** Any spending that can't be justified in terms of clear ROI is being cut in many places."

This neatly encapsulates a major problem in the marketing function. Investing in campaigns *because* they can be measured is the wrong order of operations. We should invest in campaigns that meet the needs of the business and are aligned with our goals.

Earlier in this book we referenced the John Wanamaker quote, "Half the money I spend on advertising is wasted; I just don't know which half." We've heard this dropped into meetings in response to a question about the ROI of marketing investments. And it often works—everyone has a chuckle and the conversation moves on. Wanamaker's comment is a good characterization of one challenge of measuring MROI, but it isn't a reason not to try. Also, Wanmaker died in 1922. We can't use it as an excuse forever, and we can't just shrug our shoulders and fly blind.

On the other hand, the most dangerously misinterpreted quote in marketing (sometimes attributed to Drucker, sometimes to Deming, sometimes to Ridgeway—we settled on Deming) is, "What gets measured gets managed." The reason it's dangerous is that this is only half of his quote, and consequently it is misinterpreted as being an instruction. People think we *should* manage by what we *can* measure, and by implication, *not* manage that which is difficult to measure. To make that point more explicitly, there is significant business risk in excluding from decision-making those criteria which are difficult to quantify with precision. The full text of Deming's quote, sadly not usually provided in its entirety, makes a completely different point:

> "What gets measured gets managed - **even when it's pointless to measure and manage it, and even if it harms the purpose of the organization to do so.**"

Here's an example of that. Earlier in Dan's career, he delivered technology that could automate a large number of customer service calls quickly, meaning they didn't need to be handled by a costly customer service agent. Many of his customers, contact center leaders, would insist the only metric they cared about was reducing Average Call Handle Time (ACHT), the average duration of a phone call into the contact center. He would discuss this with them and suggest there must be other things that mattered, such as successful call outcomes, customer experience, overall cost savings and so on. But some customers insisted it was only about ACHT. When this happened, he would ask why they didn't answer all their calls and then immediately hang up on their customers without talking to them. They'd achieve fantastic ACHT that way. The reason they didn't do that was because they *knew* that would be a terrible business decision. The problem is, they were being managed by what could easily be measured. What they really wanted to do was to reduce ACHT while maintaining those other benefits like first-call resolution or customer satisfaction that they found much more difficult to measure reliably.

This is therefore a cautionary tale: beware of organizing around potentially irrelevant metrics. As Igor Ansoff noted, "Managers start off trying to manage what they want, and finish up wanting what they can measure."

The marketing function contains a fantastic example of this: we started off wanting to measure and tune our marketing investments and mix, and we finished up with the pseudo-science of marketing attribution models.

Are these our only options then? Wanamaker's world, in which we fly blind and accept the inherent inefficiency of our activities, or Deming's, in which we labor under the false precision of managing merely by what we can measure while under-valuing things we know to be critical, but which are difficult to measure? No. We can do much better.

Part of doing better is measuring at the right level. The right level means a level where ROI really makes sense, both within and outside of, marketing. Measuring the ROI of a white paper is not useful. Measuring the ROI of investments into a product launch is. So before we dive into MROI measurements, let's first address the levels of marketing measurement, and how to select the right one for your needs.

The four levels of marketing measurement

Despite becoming increasingly digital and data-driven, marketers still struggle more than their counterparts in other corporate functions to communicate the business impact of their work in a consistent way. Marketing performance metrics should be regularly tracked to measure success and gauge whether goals are being met.

There is clarity to be gained in defining a framework that introduces marketing-measurement levels. The tools and outputs of each level are different, and they add value at different stages in the marketing funnel. Said another way, they answer different questions for marketers. It is important to match your question to the appropriate level of measurement or you will get incomplete, or even misleading, results back. The levels of measurement are:

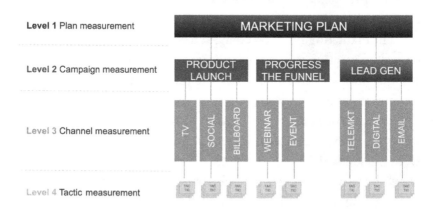

Please note that here, in Level 2, campaign refers to a thematic campaign (a product launch, a thought leadership campaign, a funnel nurturing campaign) that may encompass multiple channels.

These levels are useful for answering different types of questions. In general, as you move down the levels toward tactical measurement, the more specialized and narrow the marketing performance metrics will be (e.g., click-through rate, whitepaper download count, intra-channel content optimization, even cost per click).

As you move up toward plan measurement, the results tend to be more strategic and business-oriented (i.e., less specific to marketing alone), and the easier it is to communicate those metrics to non-marketing colleagues (e.g., "What's our plan ROI?" or "Which campaigns are performing best?").

If we try to measure whether we have identified the best message for our audience using the channel as the measurement level, we can only really answer the question for a given channel. It's true that the expression of a message and audience is shaped by the channel, but the correctness of the overall audience and message selection must be measured at the campaign level and then tuned for delivery over each channel.

Example: Imagine a credit card marketing campaign with the goal to encourage people who travel a lot to switch from their current card to the new ACME card. The campaign message broadcast over the TV channel ("ACME card gives you double points for hotel bookings, and you can convert the points to air miles") is different from the message for the direct mail channel ("Congratulations Mrs. Nguyen, you've been pre-approved for an ACME card. Fill in the application form and get 6 months 0% interest on any balance transferred"). These are different messaging elements of a broader campaign messaging strategy. If we only measure at the channel level, or we measure channel-first (versus campaign-first) we are going to only see a part of the picture. If we measure at the campaign level, we can draw the threads from disparate channels together into a more informative, complete measurement of performance.

Sometimes you may even harm your marketing insight overall if you try to answer the question by measuring at the incorrect level.

Example: A credit union is trying to increase the proportion of its members who take out a car loan with them. They implement a campaign over billboards, print ads, local radio ads, and digital. A channel-first measurement approach will attempt to work out the independent contributions of each channel. But how do you measure how much billboards contributed versus print ads versus digital? And how do you tell whether someone who clicks the Facebook ad has already heard a radio ad and seen the billboard too? It's possible to spend a lot of effort gaining an incomplete view focused on just one channel instead of measuring results in aggregate at the campaign level and asking the question, "Did more people sign up for auto-loans after we executed the campaign?" That is the first-order question.

You may notice that measuring channel-first is suboptimal for a number of common and important questions. As a practical matter, it's important for marketers to understand what is best measured channel-first. Since there is a channel-first structure in many organizations, that can inadvertently lead to trying to answer too many, or the wrong kind of, questions with channel-level measurement.

Channel-oriented measurement: Its popularity and potential pitfalls

Consider a few of the key marketing channels: TV, radio, print, billboard, digital, social media, and events. The tools, skills, consultant and agency networks, platforms, reports, etc. that are needed to orchestrate and run campaigns via these channels are quite different from each other.

It is not surprising, therefore, that individuals tend to become experts in executing campaigns over a subset of the channels. Events managers rarely also run digital campaigns, and vice versa. As we illustrated earlier in the book, this reality leads to teams being built around channel expertise, and since budget allocations tend to follow team structure, many marketing teams allocate budget by channel.

In a channel-oriented team structure, individual performance is likely to be managed by the performance of the channel. Team members naturally become focused on the performance of their channel. They want to dedicate funds to that channel. They prioritize reporting on how that channel is performing.

Furthermore, there are specialized, channel-specific tools, reports, and metrics for measuring performance within a channel that cannot possibly encompass everything that went into a campaign. For example, ad platforms report ROI based entirely on ad spend, but they don't capture the other costs that go into creating the ads.

While there are many good things to measure in a channel, unless the campaign is entirely run through one channel, those measurements do not typically tell the company whether its marketing campaigns are successful or not.

Such an orientation can lead to a local approach to marketing measurement ("Which channels are performing best/worst?" or "Is social working?") rather than a global approach ("Is this campaign achieving its target metrics and ROI?", or "Are we achieving our key goals?")

Now that we've covered the importance of measuring your marketing performance at the right level, let's talk about measuring marketing ROI accurately.

The path toward practical, valuable MROI measurement is based on four key elements:

1. Focus on big-picture, first-order ROI calculation (i.e. as we've just mentioned, measure at the right level)
2. Carefully select meaningful metrics
3. Adopt a new, consistent approach to MROI measurement across your whole marketing plan
4. Baseline and benchmark your performance

First-order ROI

Many marketers - many marketing organizations - measure second-order ROI. It is important to understand the difference between first- and second-order ROI. Below, the text in **bold** is required to measure first-order ROI. The text in italics impacts first-order ROI, but their measurement does not capture or communicate ROI.

We will invest X dollars in

- *Individual activities (write a piece of content, design a logo, hire an agency, buy some media)*
- *Which roll up to marketing messages and deliverables (digital assets, brand assets, eBooks, white papers, advertisements)*
- *Which are included in a campaign that is run (TV campaign, integrated marketing campaign, customer event)*
- *To a targeted set of customers and prospects (a market segment, installed-base customers, recent college graduates living within 10 miles of Chicago)*
- *By a target date (July 1, end of Q3)*
- *Over a defined set of marketing channels (TV, radio, digital, print)*
- *Until a certain deadline is met (ad budget is consumed, target metric achieved, Christmas)*

in order to achieve measure Y at volume Z.

First-order ROI questions ask, "Did we achieve our target measure at the desired volumes within our target budget?" and then ask whether it was worth it. For example, if we generate $1M of bookings from a campaign investment of $200,000, it's a 5x ROI. It's pretty clear that it was worth it.

Second-order ROI is replete with *did-we-do-it* (DWDI) metrics. These tend to be focused on activities rather than outcomes. They tend to be easy to measure too, which makes them *seem* attractive. But the siren song of DWDI metrics is foiled by the fact that they don't tell you anything about the business outcome of your campaign.

If you ask a colleague how their campaign went and you hear an answer like, "It launched on time with finalized positioning, and all the digital assets were completed by the agency, to spec," they might be giving you DWDI metrics. What you really want to hear is something more like, "We've used 90% of our budget and we've achieved 60% of our Sales-Qualified Lead (SQL) target so far, which puts us ahead of schedule. We're forecasting that we'll overperform with this campaign." then you are likely tracking first order ROI metrics, because you will be able to calculate your cost per SQL, the average financial value of an SQL, and you will be able to compare it to other campaigns to assess both relative and absolute performance.

Meaningful metrics

Many marketers have written about how difficult it can be to assess the ROI impact of marketing activities higher up the funnel, such as social media likes. Earlier in this book, we covered the importance of goals-based marketing. We argue that there are really only three overarching objectives to marketing activity: improving sales, awareness, or perception.

Based on that, below is a table showing the most common marketing goals, and how to measure success—both the measure (number, percentage) and the unit of measurement (customers, deals, lead).

Key metrics for common marketing goals
Note: LPO = lead, prospect or opportunity

Sales-Driven Goals	How to Measure Success	Measure	Unit
Acquire new customers	Count net new customer wins	Number	Customer
Reduce customer churn	% change of customers that stay vs. leave	Percentage	Customer
Increase revenue	New revenue - old revenue	Number	Currency
Upsell/cross-sell customers	Count the number of marketing-sourced up/cross-sells	Number	Deal
Create marketing-sourced revenue	Sum the revenue originated by marketing	Number	Currency
Create marketing-influenced revenue	Sum the revenue influenced by marketing	Number	Currency
Create marketing-sourced opportunities	Count the number of opportunities by marketing	Number	LPO
Generate marketing-sourced leads	Count the number of leads	Number	LPO
Build/grow a contact database	Count the number of new contacts	Number	LPO
Grow a new sales channel	Sum the indirect channel revenue	Number	Currency
Reduce sales cycle time	Average time of all deals from lead to close compared to average time from previous period	Number	Day
Grow market share through competitive replacement	% increase, determined by survey or reported revenue	Percentage	Currency
Expand into new markets (by geo, demo, industry, size)	Count number of customers in new markets	Number	Customer
Retain customers	Customer retention %	Percentage	Customer

Awareness-Driven Goals	How to Measure Success	Measure	Unit
Improve awareness	Count Impressions, articles, social mentions, etc. and compare to previous period	Number	Views
Increase web traffic	Count the # of visitors on your website and compare to previous period	Percentage	Views
Launch a new initiative	Coverage in press (count # of mentions)	Number	Mentions
Launch a new product or solution	Coverage in press (count # of mentions)	Number	Mentions
Educate external audiences	Downloads/views of content	Number	Views
Generate Twitter followers	Count the followers	Number	Person
Generate LinkedIn connections	Count the connections	Number	Person
Generate Facebook friends	Count the friends	Number	Person
Obtain news coverage (PR)	Count the articles	Number	Articles
Grow share of voice	Percent of articles you generate vs. competition compared to previous period	Percentage	Articles
Create more speaking opportunities	Count the # opportunities and the attendance compared to previous period	Number	Views
Build an industry analyst program	Count the # of mentions by analysts	Percentage	Mentions
Grow content marketing program	Count the # of pieces of content and compare to previous period	Number	Articles

Perception-Driven Goals	How to Measure Success	Measure	Unit
Increase customer satisfaction	% growth in CSAT, NPS, survey, etc. compared to previous period	Percentage	Change
Increase customer evangelism	% growth in # of case studies, speaking opps, etc. compared to previous period	Percentage	Change
Rebrand or re-position	% of survey who report desired perception compared to previous period	Percentage	Person
Refine/change messaging	% of survey who report desired perception compared to previous period	Percentage	Person
Become a thought leader	Count the number of content views compared to previous period	Number	Person

Continuous versus Binary Metrics

You may have noticed that 100% of the metrics above are continuous, meaning they're countable, have no upper bound, and they're not binary (answered by yes/no).

Binary criteria are indicative of DWDI metrics (Did we launch on time? Was the collateral written? Did we approve the agency's recommendations?) DWDI metrics often belong in a project plan, but they normally do not belong in your ROI analysis.

Metrics Categories

You may also have noticed in the table above that the number of different types of units to be measured is rather limited. This means that there are relatively few things to measure to get to the core of your ROI calculations. It's not necessarily easy to measure them all the time, but it's important to know the universe within which you're operating.

As the list below illustrates, the only units of measurement that are required to assess the large spread of typical marketing goals can be captured by the 10 following units of measurement.

Number of articles

Number of customers

Number of leads (or prospects or opportunities, depending on your definitions)

Currency amount (revenue, bookings, pipeline)

Number of days (deal cycle)

Number of deals (new win, upsell, cross-sell)

Number of mentions

Percentage change (growth- NPS score or decline-churn rate)

Number of people (survey or focus group respondents, social network connections)

Number of views (pages, articles, white papers, gated downloads)

Prioritizing just 10 units of measurement is simplifying. And to put a finer point on it, there are five units for sales goals, four for awareness goals, and just two for perception goals.

Sales Driven Goals	Awareness Driven Goals	Perception Driven Goals
% or # of Customers	% or # of People	% or # of People
% or # of LPO	% or # of Views	% Change in Perception
% or # of Deals	% or # of Mentions	
% or # of Days in deal cycle	% or # of Articles	
% or sum of Currency Amount		

While we don't claim this is an exhaustive list of all possible marketing metrics to inform first-order ROI, if you set up systems to measure these, and they're tied to well-structured goals, then you are well positioned to capture first-order ROI metrics for a meaningful proportion of your marketing efforts.

Tying metrics to ROI

Now that we have our goals and we've selected metrics to measure those goals, we need to establish the value of those metrics. What is it worth to achieve one of the outcomes tied to our metrics?

Some of these are simple. For example, currency amount may be mapped to revenue, bookings or pipeline. For the sake of simplicity, let's assume that the revenue we generate is exactly equivalent to the customer's lifetime value (LTV). Hopefully it won't be the case that LTV is equal to one-time revenue, but it helps keep things simple for now.

If you know the conversion rates for our pipeline and bookings, then it is easy to map metrics to business value. Let's imagine that there is a 10% conversion rate of pipeline to revenue, and 95% of bookings to revenue. Then, you can state that:

$1,000,000 of revenue = $1,000,000 of business value
$1,000,000 of bookings = $950,000 of business value
$1,000,000 of pipeline = $100,000 of business value

Spending $100,000 to generate $1,000,000 of revenue or bookings is a pretty great investment. Spending that much to generate $1,000,000 of pipeline is a pretty terrible investment, because the best possible outcome is the same as the investment. And the outcome is not guaranteed. So, you'd be better off spending the $100,000 on something else.

We started with revenue because it represents the most direct connection to your marketing investment. Some metrics are closer to revenue, and some are farther away.

Adopt a new, consistent approach to MROI

It's important to adopt a consistent approach to MROI measurement, both for campaigns and for an entire marketing plan. Once you have achieved that, you can create a reliable benchmark for your marketing organization's performance, both to assess relative performance changes over time, and to compare your performance to similar organizations.

Three key principles of MROI

Earlier in Dan's career, he worked for an acquisitive company. They acquired over 100 companies during his tenure there. Barely a day passed without some kind of due diligence meeting somewhere in the company. In one of those meetings, the CEO of a company they were assessing complained that they were undervaluing some of his company's technology. He said that they were too focused on the P&L and were overlooking the "strategic value" of these assets. One of Dan's colleagues challenged the CEO to describe a strategic value that didn't ultimately show up on the P&L—either as a revenue or margin benefit. The CEO wasn't able to.

What the CEO meant when he said "strategic value" was that that financial benefit was uncertain and a long way in the future. With some modeling, all the "strategic" programs his company was carrying out could be projected into the future to tell us when the benefit should start to arrive. A sensitivity analysis could be carried out on what the potential range of outcomes might be. Then, based on time and risk, they could discount the value of those benefits and attempt to quantify the value in the present day. They couldn't do it with total precision, and they didn't agree on some of the variables, but they weren't flying blind.

Marketing plans and campaigns offer up a similar opportunity— they yield financial outcomes, and they may deliver value far in the future. These are two of the fundamental principles that you will need to support in order to be able to measure the true ROI of your marketing plan and its campaigns. If you don't apply these concepts, it is difficult to measure the true ROI of marketing activities.

Key Principle #1: All marketing campaigns have an ultimate, quantifiable, financial target

Many marketers carry out their campaigns and then try to figure out retrospectively what the ROI was. This is backwards. It is more effective to identify your target financial outcome (your return), and use that to inform how much you will spend on marketing to reach your target (your investment). Of course, you can *only* do that if you identify your desired financial outcome.

It's obvious that a lead generation campaign has a financial outcome: identify and create leads that become prospects, then opportunities, then customers. Other types of marketing campaigns might present a less obvious path to a financial outcome. For example, a rebranding campaign might seem like something that isn't directly tied to revenue. But, if you think in terms of where our campaign is affecting the funnel, and then follow the funnel to its end, there is *always* a financial outcome. From this angle, it's clear that a rebranding campaign has a financial objective, it's just farther up the funnel and farther away in time from the financial outcome of increased sales. For a commercial company (versus a non-profit) the question is, What marketing campaign would not have a financial motivation?

When thinking about ROI for your campaigns, it is important to zoom out far enough so that you can draw a line from the marketing activities of today to the financial outcomes of that activity through the funnel. Then you can get a sense for what the future looks like for your company if you do those activities or not. This brings us to the second fundamental point: time.

Key Principle #2: MROI is not tied to the fiscal year

Your budget begins on the first day of the fiscal year, but your plan doesn't. Imagine your fiscal year matches the calendar year. On January 1, your pipeline is not empty. There are people in the world aware of your brand. Leads, prospects and opportunities exist at various stages in the funnel. Deals are being actively negotiated by sales. Marketing campaigns are underway from the previous fiscal year.

This means that some proportion of your marketing results for the fiscal year are already in the bag. From the perspective of this year's budget, they feel free. But they were obviously funded from last year's budget. It would be unrealistic to make a plan that did not fully take into account these carried over benefits from extant campaigns.

It would obviously be disastrous for your business if you only executed campaigns to create value in the current fiscal year. It would also be extremely difficult to do.

It's important that your marketing organization, and your company's executive team, embrace the notion that different campaigns have different value horizons and treat campaign investments as just that—*investments* with a return in the future. The marketing team's job is to ensure there is a well-calibrated number of well-qualified opportunities for sales to close at all times, which entails working a marketing funnel that will usually operate out of step with the fiscal year.

Key Principle #3: Every phase of the funnel is worth the same as the financial target

If you have a revenue target of $1M for a campaign, and you need to close 10 deals to achieve that revenue target, it's obvious that those 10 deals are worth $100,000 each, on average. Let's step back one phase in the marketing funnel, and stipulate that you need to have 20 qualified opportunities in order to get to 10 deals. What are those 20 qualified opportunities worth? $1M. This is not an additional $1M, it's the *same* $1M, because hidden in those 20 qualified deals are the 10 deals that will ultimately close. Another way of saying this is that it's the same 10 deals at every stage of the pipeline, always worth $1M. The job of the marketing campaigns through the funnel is to find them, and filter out the rest.

So let's keep going back, and say that you need 100 prospects to create 20 qualified opportunities. 100 prospects, collectively, are worth the same $1M. If you need 1,000 leads to get to 100 prospects, then 1,000 leads are worth $1M. You can't achieve the revenue target without the preceding funnel targets being hit. 1,000 leads contain 100% of the value of the sources of the financial target, plus a lot of leads that need to be filtered out through the marketing funnel and put into some nurturing campaign or lost. Every phase of the funnel - if its targets are achieved - is worth exactly the same as the final revenue outcome. This is a useful thing to bear in mind when you're asked to identify the value of top-of-the-funnel marketing activities. If you understand your funnel and conversion metrics, you should be able to quantify it.

Viewed this way, we can assert that, for this example, a deal is worth $100,000 ($1M/10); a qualified opportunity is worth $50,000 ($1M/20), a prospect is worth $10,000 ($1M/100), and a lead is worth $1,000 ($1M/1000). This is a crucial point to measure ROI consistently, and to be able to properly value marketing outcomes in the earlier stages of the marketing funnel.

Prerequisites for the MROI model

Here are some questions you need to answer before you can calculate ROI consistently:

Will you measure return in terms of revenue or margin?

Either may make sense depending on your business at a given point in time, but each will yield considerably different ROIs from the other.

What is your financial unit of measurement?

Ultimately, it should be money, usually expressed as revenue. This may be one-time customer revenue, lifetime value, a percentage of LTV, and so on. Using one-time revenue for a one-time purchase obviously makes sense. For recurring revenue deals, some share of LTV makes sense.

Example: Your average deal size is $10K annual recurring revenue. Your average customer retention rate is five years. LTV is therefore $50K. If you use $10K in your ROI valuation, you will end up with an artificially low ROI. If you use $50K, it will be unrealistically high. 50% of LTV may be a reasonable measure to use in ROI calculation once you've considered the cost of customer support and renewals after the customer is acquired.

What is your target ROI multiple?

If you are seeking a 5x ROI and you have a clearly defined financial outcome, then you can easily back into the implied marketing budget for a campaign, and an entire plan. Doing it this way gives you the chance to assess the feasibility of a campaign. Does it seem achievable to reach your target outcome with the implied investment at your target ROI? That might save you from embarking on campaigns that have a low likelihood of achieving their outcome from day one.

Note: You should not complicate the ROI model with time-value of money calculations such as net present value (NPV). There is enough uncertainty in the execution of the campaign over time. Time-value of money calculations in this context lend a false precision that is not worth the complexity.

The most important thing is that when you determine what you will use as inputs to the model, you stick with them for a long enough period to compare results over time, and across campaigns.

Worked Example of Marketing ROI calculation

In this example, we're going to model a marketing ROI based on an integrated campaign to secure 50 new customers for a SaaS product. The average 1-year contract value is $10,000, and the typical customer retention rate is 6 years, yielding an LTV of $60,000. The business has an 80% gross margin.

After factoring in retention and renewal costs after the initial sale, the marketing team calculates that each lead is worth 50% of the LTV of the customer. The targeted return is therefore:

Return = 50 deals * 60,000 LTV * 80% GM * 50%
value attribution
Return = $1,200,000

The team has a target ROI of 4, meaning their marketing investments should return 4 times the investment. The Marketing ROI calculation is as follows:

ROI = ($1,200,000 - Investment)/Investment
4 = ($1,200,000 - Investment)/Investment

We can calculate the investment that would achieve this ROI at this target outcome as follows:

$$ROI = (\$1,200,000 - Investment)/Investment$$
$$4 = (\$1,200,000 - Investment)/Investment$$
$$4 * Investment = \$1,200,000 - Investment$$
$$4 * Investment + Investment = \$1,200,000$$
$$5 * Investment = \$1,200,000$$
$$Investment = \$1,200,000/5$$
$$Investment = \$240,000$$

In principle, if you spend $240,000 and are successful in achieving your financial target, you will have achieved an ROI of 4. Now you must enter your funnel conversion metrics for each phase of your funnel and determine what top-of-funnel and mid-funnel programs need to be run.

Here are the results for our worked example (your numbers may vary):

	Conversion Metrics	Implied Need
Leads	20%	4175
Prospects	40%	835
Opportunities	15%	334
Deals		50

If we need 50 deals, then based on conversion metrics we can estimate that we need 334 opportunities, 835 prospects and so on, up the funnel. If we change our assumptions about conversion rates or target outcomes, then the implied needs further up the funnel will change accordingly. If you don't know the specific conversion metrics for your organization, it is better to do some research and make an educated guess than to not use them at all. By observing the results of past campaigns, it should be possible to at least land in the right ballpark.

You may recall our third principle of MROI earlier, that every phase of the funnel has the same value as the target outcome. Based on this, we can ascribe a value to every funnel outcome by dividing the funnel value by the number of outcomes required at each phase in the funnel.

Funnel Phase	Conversion Rate	Outcomes needed in each Funnel Phase	Value of Funnel Phase	Value per Outcome
Lead Conversion	20%	4,175 leads	$ 1,200,000	$ 287
Prospect Conversion	40%	835 prospects	$ 1,200,000	$ 1,437
Opportunity Conversion	15%	334 opportunities	$ 1,200,000	$ 3,593
Target Outcome		50 deals	$ 1,200,000	$ 24,000

Finally, we need to decide how much of our marketing budget we're going to invest into each phase of the funnel. This is something that frequently does not occur as it should. It's a common mistake to treat each phase in the funnel as its own discrete entity rather than as part of the larger engine which culminates in a target financial outcome.

The team will rely on its sales force to do most of the conversion from Opportunity to Deal. So it will only invest 2% of its budget into the last phase. It also knows from experience that it is relatively low cost to nurture leads through the middle of the funnel, so it dedicates 11% to convert prospects to opportunities, and 12% to convert leads to prospects. That leaves the remaining 75% for getting the leads into the top of the funnel.

Here's what the funnel phases look like with this distribution of campaign budget:

	LEADS →	PROSPECTS →	OPPORTUNITIES →	CLOSED DEALS
Share of campaign budget	71%	12%	11%	2%
Marketing investment	$180,000	$28,800	$26,400	$4,800

Note that the total marketing budget sums up to our target $240,000 budget to achieve $1,200,000 of target financial benefit at a 4x ROI

As the campaign is executed, we can calculate the ROI of each phase cumulatively through the funnel, as follows:

	LEADS →	PROSPECTS →	OPPORTUNITIES →	CLOSED DEALS
Share of campaign budget	75%	12%	11%	2%
Marketing investment	$ 180,000	$ 28,800	$ 26,400	$ 4,800
TARGET outcome	4,175	835	334	50
ACTUAL outcome	3,976	790	380	55
Value per outcome	$ 287.43	$ 1,437.13	$ 3,593	$ 24,000
TARGET Funnel Value	$ 1,200,000	$ 1,200,000	$ 1,200,000	$ 1,200,000
ACTUAL Funnel Value	$ 1,142,882	$ 1,135,329	$ 1,365,269	$ 1,344,000
TARGET ROI (cumulative)	5.67	4.75	4.10	4.00
ACTUAL ROI (cumulative)	5.40	4.49	4.67	4.48
ROI as % of TARGET	95%	95%	114%	112%

To understand this table, let's look at the leftmost section, called LEADS, which represents the first phase of the campaign.

You can see that 75% of the budget has been allocated to this phase, which represents $180,000 of the available budget for the campaign. The target outcome is 4,175 leads. Because the value of the funnel is constant, you can calculate a value per lead of $287.43.

Unfortunately, when you look at the actual outcome of this phase of the campaign (in bold), you can see that it fell short, and only generated 3,976 leads. If you multiply out your value/ outcome, that shows a funnel value of $1.14M rather than the target of $1.20M.

Because you're dealing in real numbers, you can also calculate a target and actual ROI value for this phase of the campaign. Here, you've achieved an ROI of 5.4 versus the target ROI of 5.67 for this phase. Why does the ROI change as we proceed through the funnel? Because while the *value* of the funnel remains constant at $1.2M, your *investment* changes at each stage as you consume more of the budget. So the target ROI for top-of-the-funnel phases will always be higher than the ROI for late-stage phases. It may seem counterintuitive, but it has to be the case if you follow a campaign ROI all the way through the funnel to a target financial outcome.

Although the campaign got off to a shaky start, you can see that you actually leave the 3rd phase of the funnel ahead of plan, and the team is able to close more deals than originally targeted, meaning that the overall campaign exceeds the target ROI—you aimed for an ROI of 4.0 and achieved an ROI of 4.48, 112% of target. Here's a visualization of how the program evolved through the phases:

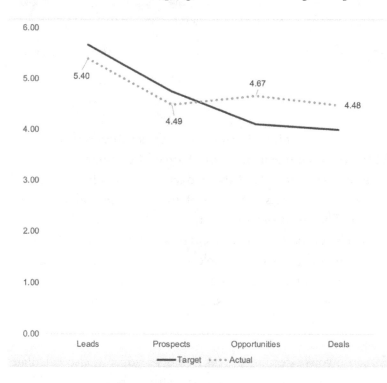

ROI evolution through the funnel

The actual ROI (dotted line) started off short of the target, but ended up overtaking the target and beating expectations. The next time a similar campaign is to be run, the marketing team should assess whether their assumptions about conversion metrics at different stages of the funnel were wrong, or whether this was just natural variance that can't be controlled for.

The next chart, below, shows how the campaign performed as a percentage of target ROI at each stage in the funnel. This allows the team to understand whether they have performance issues they need to address, and to ask themselves whether they staffed and sourced the campaign optimally.

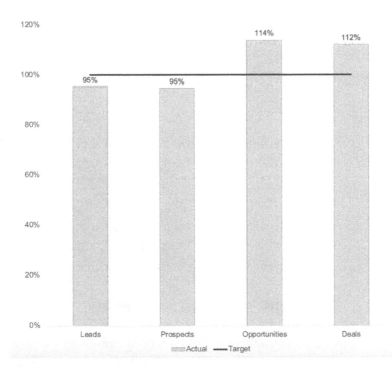

ROI achievement through the funnel

Finally, we can see the evolution of the funnel value (the number of outcomes multiplied by the value per outcome). This shows that our funnel value ended up ahead of our target financial outcome, and this is what drove our ROI to be even better than the targeted

ROI of 4. Note that the target financial outcome remains constant throughout the campaign. That is one of the principles of calculating the true ROI of the campaign.

Value evolution through funnel phases

The approach above applies to any marketing campaign—churn reduction, account-based marketing, cross-sell and upsell, and so on. It also allows you to zoom out your ROI perspective and to pull together various marketing activities that cohere into a target financial outcome.

For example, it may not seem like a positioning program and a meeting generation program are part of the same effort initially, but they actually are different phases of the same overarching campaign to reach a financial target. As such, the entire ROI for that marketing funnel should be measured as a whole, both on a return and an investment level.

Baselines and benchmark your performance

It is important to understand how your campaigns are performing in absolute terms, meaning that you have an understanding of whether a given campaign is contributing what is needed to meet your defined targets.

It is also critical to measure relative performance over time. Is the team as a whole improving, holding steady, or declining, from an MROI perspective? Are there certain individuals whose campaigns overperform consistently? By maintaining a consistent approach to MROI across campaigns and over time, you can more effectively assess and communicate these measures.

There are several reasons why it is worth taking a different approach to MROI and applying it consistently across all of your marketing activities:

1. You can place all marketing campaigns into the context of financial outcomes. If you find that you can't do that - if there is no path from a marketing activity to a financial outcome - then you should question whether that marketing activity is a priority.
2. You can communicate to your team and to the broader organization when and how different types of marketing will yield a benefit, and be able to frame how something that may seem difficult to quantify (such as downloads of a thought leadership piece) is actually an event that carries a specific monetary value.
3. You can measure the performance of individuals on your team based on a constant funnel value. Even if the overall

campaign is not successful, you will be able to see who was able to deliver on their phase of the campaign and who was not.

4. You can organize what may initially seem like disparate marketing activities into coherent campaigns that culminate in a specific target financial outcome.

5. You can better justify your marketing budget, and better justify your requests for greater investment.

6. You can make quicker, better decisions on which marketing activities to adjust, or curtail, based on the ROI forecast against the target funnel value.

7. You can benchmark performance across campaigns, individuals, and against historical results.

CHAPTER 11

How to Present Marketing Results to Your CEO and Board

After presenting marketing results hundreds of times to boards, CEOs, and senior executive teams, we started to see some patterns develop regarding the expectations from these audiences. More recently, marketing leaders have not been able to get away with presenting high-level information, selective results, or lists of projects and activities. These leaders are being held to a high standard of operational rigor and are expected to present their results in the context of the business.

Considerations for presenting to CEOs, board members, and other senior executives

When developing your presentation for an executive audience, it's important to shift your mindset from that of a practitioner of marketing who is in promotional mode to a leader of a critical business function who is reporting facts in the context of the business. Successfully making that shift is a critical requirement for marketing leaders. The list below is a good test to see if you have made that transition:

- Focus on results, not activities
- Show the relationship to your goals
- Communicate value in business terms, not marketing terms
- Provide context for results
- Be consistent with your reporting format and content
- Tell the truth
- Tell the WHOLE truth
- Take the opportunity to teach, but not preach

Focus on results, not activities

This may seem rough, but your CEO doesn't care how you have been filling your day. She really wants to know about the outcomes. Many marketing leaders fall into the trap of delivering an activity report instead of the business results achieved.

The table below contrasts results reporting with activity reporting:

Results (Share these!)	Activities (Nobody cares.)
• Generated $2M in incremental pipeline • Positive article in *NY Times* reflecting our industry views • Identified 20 customer expansion opportunities for new product	• Wrote 24 blog posts • Ran a seminar series in 3 cities • Delivered 2,345,124 emails

Notice that in the results column, the list includes a few different kinds of outcomes, including pipeline generation, press coverage, and opportunity identification. The column on the right may represent a lot of work performed by your team, but it is not useful for your executive team to know about unless you can connect these activities to the outcomes. For example, you could say that your team "ran a seminar series in 3 cities that generated 6 new customer expansion opportunities representing $800k in new pipeline."

Show the relationship to your goals

While reporting in the form of results is necessary, it doesn't communicate the entire story. If we take the example of the results above, each bullet begs the question, "How does this compare to our goals?"

A more complete communication of the results would add a comparison to your targets, as shown in the examples below:

- Generated $2M in incremental pipeline in Q2 **vs. target of $1.8M (111%)**
- Positive article in *NY Times* reflecting our industry views **vs. target of 2 major news outlets reflecting our position (50%)**
- Identified 20 customer expansion opportunities for our new product in Q2 **vs. target of 10 (200%) as part of our customer expansion efforts**

Notice that the comparison to the goals tells a much more complete picture of achievement. In the first and third examples above, the performance was well ahead of plan. The PR coverage in the *NY Times*, while exciting, did not meet the target.

It may feel uncomfortable to highlight the fact that you did not achieve the objective, but it's more comfortable than having to respond to a board member who asks how this compares to your goals when they are not listed.

Communicate value in business terms, not marketing terms

While this recommendation is important for all audiences, it is especially important when presenting to board members. Board members rarely have backgrounds in marketing, with the majority of them coming from financial backgrounds.

Take a look at the table below, which compares the communication of business results versus marketing buzzwords:

Business Results (Good!)	Marketing Buzzwords (Bad!)
• Generated $2M in incremental pipeline, expected to convert to $450,000 of incremental revenue based on historical conversion rates	• Email campaigns delivered 14.5% CTR • Created 4,000 MQLs in Q2

The examples above highlight two major factors that will improve your communication: connection to a business outcome and connection to the English language. The first example not only uses a metric (pipeline) that will be universally understood by the audience, but it tells the complete story by highlighting how this interim result is expected to convert to business value over time.

The examples in the righthand column use marketing jargon ("CTR" or click-through rate, and "MQLs" or marketing qualified leads) and do not show the connection to business value. To improve the last example, you could define your terms and add some business context by saying "We created 4,000 marketing qualified leads (MQL) in Q2, which are expected to generate 100 new opportunities (2.5% historical conversion rate), representing $2.5M in incremental pipeline at $25K ACV."

While that example may seem verbose, it includes the necessary context to explain the business value of the result.

Provide context for your results

We've all seen marketers proudly report on a metric to senior management and then pause, waiting for the thunderous applause, only to instead find they've just created an awkward pause in their presentation. That's the moment the marketer learns that his or her audience does not have the framework to understand that the results are exceptional.

Providing context for your audience can take on one of the following forms:

- **Showing results compared to your goals or with a direct connection to a business result:** (Described above).
- **Using an external benchmark:** For example, you could say, "Our improved sales tools increased the conversion rate of our funnel from 14% to 17% versus the standard for our industry of 15%." This assumes that external benchmarks are available, which is not always the case.
- **Using an internal benchmark:** If an external benchmark is not available for your metric, it can be helpful to compare your result to an internal benchmark. The same result above could be expressed with the context of an internal comparison as follows: "Our improved sales tools increased the conversion rate of our funnel from 14% to 17% versus our previous best conversion rate of 16%."
- **Trending data:** Another strategy to communicate context is to visually show the progression of your metric over time. For example, if you were trying to communicate the performance of your campaign measured by qualified leads, rather than describing the progress with words, you could share a chart like the one below. It shows how you are progressing toward your target, or in the case below where

we are trending ahead of our target (from our own internal campaign at Plannuh, measured by Plannuh).

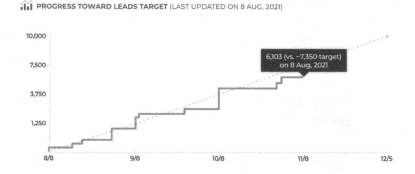

PROGRESS TOWARD LEADS TARGET (LAST UPDATED ON 8 AUG, 2021)

Be consistent with your reporting format and content

Ideally, the presentation of your marketing results should be easy for the reader to understand. But any complex set of information takes some time to fully understand it. This is one of the reasons why we recommend that you maintain a consistent format for presenting your results.

Remember that your audience reviews this data infrequently, and they often consume lots of different kinds of information, including financial information, sales reports, research and development updates, operations data, and more. It will be far easier for your audience to understand the data if you use the same format each time you present your results. Ultimately, you will spend far less time explaining the format of the data and more time discussing the implications of the results.

The other reason why consistency is important is that it reduces the likelihood of cherry-picking your results, which can lead to much broader issues (more on this in the section titled, "Tell the WHOLE truth").

Tell the truth

Some marketers spend their entire careers learning to use words and data to create their own version of reality. It is critical that you remember that when you are presenting your business results, your job is to tell the truth, not spin the results to make you or your team look good.

Why is this important? First of all, in this setting, you are using data to make business decisions about the application and prioritization of resources. If your big campaign concept didn't deliver on expectations, your job is to explain the results, along with your analysis of what happened. You should then be prepared to make a recommendation about resources. Is it still worth it to proceed with this campaign? Are there changes that should be made? Would it be better to shift the resources to another campaign, or even to another department? If you aren't honest about the results, you won't be able to make the right recommendations to improve your business outcome.

There is another reason why telling the truth is important: Trust. The highest functioning management teams trust each other. And not telling the truth is one of the fastest ways to erode trust in the team. Here's an example that illustrates the value of trust.

A CMO at a large company also had the responsibility of acting as the general manager for a direct-to-consumer software business. The head of marketing for that team was incredibly bright and creative, and the CEO and CFO often came to the CMO to find new ways to generate growth for the company. They had been selling their software via our ecommerce site and via retail, but the head of consumer marketing thought they should try to set up demonstration kiosks in shopping malls for the holiday season. They modeled out the investment (which was millions of dollars) and highlighted the risks. In this case, they were wrong about the effectiveness of the model. And even though they were tempted to make it look better, they were transparent with the results and recommended that they cut their losses. While the CEO and CFO weren't happy, they still trusted them. And the next time they had the opportunity to try something new, they were given that opportunity because it was clear that they would do the right thing when it came to presenting their results.

Sidebar: How to communicate bad news

As mentioned above, it is critical to communicate the truth. But it is also important to know how to communicate the truth when it involves bad news.

There are three things that you should keep in mind when you have to deliver negative news:

1. **Measure it again:** Before you start telling everyone that the sky is falling, take a breath and make sure that it is indeed falling. Check your assumptions and your calculations before you do anything else.

2. **Communicate early:** When you are sure that there is a problem, don't wait for the big meeting to drop the news. Let your management chain know when you suspect that things are going off the rails. Tell them that things are not going as expected, identify the steps you are taking to try to get back on track, and let them know when you will report back with an update.

3. **Don't surprise your boss in front of their boss:** The worst thing you can do is to report bad news to your board and break the news to your CEO at the same time. If the results don't look good, make sure you review with your direct manager as soon as possible to align your recommendations and mitigation strategies.

Tell the WHOLE truth

You probably assumed that we were done talking about the truth, but we're not. As mentioned above in the section of the article about consistent reporting format, it is critical that you provide a complete view of performance when you are reporting your results.

Some marketing leaders choose to focus on the good news part of their results rather than tell the complete story. This leads to some pretty difficult conversations when a marketing leader is called out for cherry-picking his or her results. The conversation usually goes something like this:

MARKETING EXEC: "Our amazing digital campaign delivered 2,000 leads in the quarter and had a 7X ROI."

CEO: "How much of your budget does this campaign represent?"

MARKETING EXEC: "7%."

CEO: "What happened with the other 93% of your budget?"

MARKETING EXEC: [crickets]

The point is that you need to tell the complete story of your functional performance. It is expected that you will highlight the best results, but you also learn a great deal from those campaigns that did not go well. If you hide behind the best parts of your marketing plan, the worst parts will never get better.

Some approaches you might use to tell the whole story include:

Breakdown 100% of your plan: A great way to summarize your results is to show your total discretionary marketing investment and your total results delivered. By starting with a top-down view, you won't miss anything.

Show the top AND bottom performing campaigns: If you have a lot of campaigns, one approach is to show five to ten of your top AND bottom campaigns. This will force you to highlight the lowest performing campaigns and identify corrective actions being taken to improve them.

Show a system view: Communicate marketing results like a system because it forces you to look at the end-to-end performance of the overall marketing machine. By forcing the team to assess the performance of each element of the system regularly, you never see the system fall too far out of tune.

Report results consistently: If you use the same reporting format each time, you will force yourself to report on the stuff that isn't as fun to talk about, but is necessary to understand for the overall performance of the organization.

Take the opportunity to teach, but not preach

A lot of marketers complain that their CEOs, or other executive counterparts, don't "get" marketing. If this is the case in your organization, your colleagues don't think that you "get" their function either. The highest performing companies have great depth and understanding across the executive team. With that in mind, it's important to understand your role in teaching the rest of your team about marketing.

If you follow the principles above, the rest of your team will develop a much keener understanding about the importance and impact of marketing. By connecting your plans and strategies to the overall business goals, the team will understand how marketing helps the business achieve its objectives. By communicating your results in business terms, they will be able to clearly see the value of the function, in a language that they understand. And by consistently telling the whole story, they will develop a deeper understanding of the function and will trust that you and your team are acting as responsible stewards of the company's resources.

Key questions your executive marketing reports should answer

Now that you are grounded in the key considerations for presenting marketing results to this audience, we need to turn to the specific content of the report. While every business has its unique information requirements, your marketing reports should be designed to answer the following questions:

Are we on target to achieve our goals?

How much are we spending to achieve our goals, and what is the implied cost per outcome and ROI?

What are the best and worst performing campaigns?

How much is marketing forecasting to spend overall versus the plan?

What optimizations could improve the plan's outcome?

What has changed in the market we serve?

Are we on target to achieve our goals?

The most important question to answer is whether the marketing team is going to achieve their goals. While that may seem like a simple question, presenting the data clearly requires an understanding of all the factors that were described in the first part of this chapter.

Clearly and concisely answering this question will set up the rest of the conversation around marketing performance. For example, if you are not achieving some of your goals, you should be prepared to discuss what is driving the underperformance and what specific remediations are in place to get back on track. And if it is not possible to get back on track, you need to be able to address other consequences, like a budget adjustment or complete replan.

The following chart is a good example of reporting progress against a key metric (leads) that is related to one of your goals (driving growth). The chart below shows the target (40,000 leads), the milestones (the quarterly targets indicated by dots in the dashed line), and the current progress.

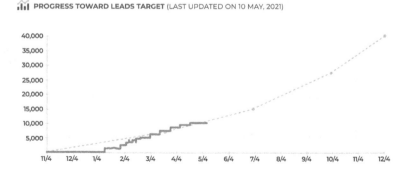

PROGRESS TOWARD LEADS TARGET (LAST UPDATED ON 10 MAY, 2021)

To provide a complete picture of performance against goals, you should include an overall assessment of each one of your goals, show the current progress versus the primary metric for each goal, and provide a forecast about future performance.

How much are we spending to achieve our goals, and what is the implied cost per outcome and ROI?

Once you have demonstrated your performance compared to your targeted outcomes, you need to show your efficiency, typically measured in spend per goal, cost per outcome (CPO) or return on investment (ROI).

The simplest measure to report is spend per goal. It gives you a high-level assessment of how you are managing your budget. As with all these metrics, spend per goal should be shown in the context of a target.

The next level of detail involves reporting on cost per outcome. For example, you may have a target cost of $50 per lead, or $1,000 per opportunity, or $0.08 per $1 of new pipeline.

The clearest way to report your results is to show the return on investment (ROI) for your goal achievement. The chart below shows the trended ROI for the same lead target above. You may have noticed that the chart is volatile in its early stages, because it is measured based on a small number of outcomes (leads). At the beginning of March, the ROI dropped to about -0.7, because the marketing team was spending money in advance of getting results. As results start to come in throughout the year, the ROI steadily increases.

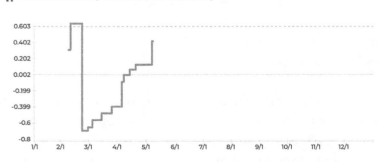

RROI ACHIEVEMENT (LAST UPDATED ON 10 MAY, 2021)

What are the best and worst performing campaigns?

The clearest way to report your best and worst performing campaigns is to show a complete ranked list of performance. If you have a large number of campaigns, that can be impractical. If that's the case, you should provide a top and bottom list of performance, including five to ten campaigns on each end of the performance scale.

There are multiple ways to measure the performance of a campaign, and it can be useful to show performance from more than one perspective. For example, you might list performance in the following ways:

> **Largest metric contribution:** Which campaigns delivered the largest number of opportunities in your pipeline?
>
> **Performance vs. forecast of metric contribution:** How did campaigns perform against. their targeted lead contribution?
>
> **Ranked CPO or ROI:** What campaigns were most efficient?

Ultimately, you want to show the campaigns that deliver performance at scale, with high efficiency.

How much is marketing forecasting to spend overall versus the plan?

An important measure of operational excellence is your ability to manage a budget. A critical component of that management is the ability to forecast your spending accurately.

The clearest way to forecast your budget is to show the spending data by status, including the expenses that have already been closed, those expenses that have been committed (via contract or PO), and finally the expenses that are planned

Using this method, (shown in the following chart) you should be able to tighten the forecast range.

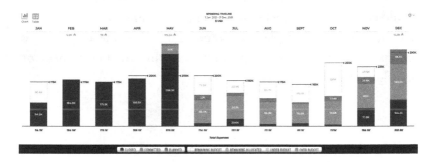

What optimizations could improve the outcome of the plan?

Once you have established a clear assessment of the performance against the plan, you should also explain any recommended adjustments that can be made to the plan to improve performance.

Your assessment should focus on the areas of highest impact. For example, you might recommend that we add another $100,000 of budget to the top-performing campaign that is also delivering a strong return on investment. Or you might recommend suspending a campaign that is performing at the bottom of the list and shifting that budget to a campaign that's performing better.

A common question that you may hear from a CEO or a board member is:

"What can you do to drive more growth?"

You should always be prepared to answer this question with a specific recommendation and assessment of the business impact, measured by cost per outcome or return on investment.

Keep in mind that if you are asked to improve performance,

the first place you should look for funding is from poor performing campaigns.

What has changed in the market we serve?

Finally, while you have the attention of the leadership team, you should communicate any important changes going on in the market that may affect your plan. Changes could include competitive actions, external factors that may impact your target customers, or significant geopolitical events.

CHAPTER 12

The Operational Marketing Index

Every marketer wants to know how they're doing in both absolute and relative terms. But there are few functions as difficult to benchmark as marketing. The diversity and disparity of measurement, and the historical difficulty in consistently measuring marketing performance, do not lend themselves to useful benchmarks.

That's why we created the Operational Marketing Index (OMI), a survey that contains a distillation of key best practices of high-performing marketing teams. Carrying out these best practices can help make you more likely to achieve successful marketing outcomes.

Of course, supporting OMI best practices does not guarantee great results for individual marketing activities or campaigns. Poor campaign execution (messaging, creative, audience selection, channel selection, etc.) will not be rescued by strong OMI performance. But having these OMI best practices in place will help you identify, measure and adapt to execution issues much more quickly, and will help improve your overall operational quality in the marketing function. For example, companies with a high OMI score will quickly identify, adjust or even end a poorly executed campaign.

OMI survey structure

Since OMI results are captured via a survey, our first challenge was to identify a list of questions that was sufficiently rich enough to accurately gauge operational excellence yet short enough that people would answer everything. We're so opinionated about this topic that we built a company around it and wrote a book to address it. Boiling that down to a manageable list of questions was no small task.

A core tenet of our model is that the marketing budget and the marketing plan must be managed together. The plan is only executable if it is affordable. The budget should be fully consumed by a goals-based plan. Having the marketing plan in one system and the marketing budget in another guarantees misalignment, inaccuracy, and confusion. With this in mind, we split the survey into two sets of questions: budget and planning questions.

Since a brief survey can't be exhaustive, we set some parameters to target the biggest bang for the buck:

1. We decided that each section should have only eight statements to respond to. We iterated our way to that number by relentlessly focusing on the highest impact questions with regard to operational excellence, and striving for a survey that was short enough that people would stick with it and provide thoughtful answers.

2. We decided that each answer should be selected from a drop-down. Our goal was to gather data from a statistically significant sample, and to afford real quantitative analysis of marketing performance instead of interview-based post-rationalization. To do that, we needed to be able to categorize responses effectively.

3. We made respondents make a choice. Our answers were set up to reflect a Likert scale gradation of responses. Likert scale surveys frequently take answers on a 5-point scale,

where the midpoint is neutral, usually with a "neither agree, nor disagree" meaning:

We did not allow that kind of answer. Respondents had to decide whether they were more positive or more negative on each of these topics. We did not believe that in reality, people would really be perfectly neutral on any of these topics. In the OMI survey, we asked survey respondents to rate their ability based on the topic of a statement, e.g., "Our marketing plan is based on a set of measurable goals that align with company objectives." Users then selected one of the following four answers:
- We don't do this
- We do some but not enough
- We do this well, but there is room for improvement
- We excel at this
4. If a respondent simply did not know whether their team did something or not, we allowed them to select that option too, rather than forcing them to provide bad data.

The final survey was conducted online.

OMI Survey Questions

There were two key sections in the survey, one focused on operational excellence in planning, and one focused on operational excellence in budget management.

Section 1: Planning questions

1. **"Our marketing plan is based on a set of measurable goals that align with company objectives."**

If you set goals, you can define what success looks like, maximize your chances of successful outcomes, baseline your performance, align the team's activities around the most important tasks, avoid random acts of marketing, and make wiser investment decisions (again, plan and budget are inextricably linked). If you align your marketing goals with corporate goals, then you are able to more easily demonstrate the business value that your marketing plan has delivered, in terms that make sense to the business.

2. **"We create comprehensive campaigns (thematic, integrated, etc.) to execute our strategies and achieve our goals."**

It's important to organize your activities into thematic campaigns with defined goals, audiences, messaging, and offers, and then to implement those campaigns over the right mix of channels. A channel-first approach will likely yield less successful campaign outcomes than a campaign-first approach.

3. **"We do scenario planning so we can quickly react to market dynamics or internal business factors."**

The best marketing teams carry out scenario analysis to pre-plan for certain circumstances. Then, they can react quickly if the need arises. For example, how would you adjust the marketing plan if you had 20% more budget, or 20% less? Developing and modeling out what-if scenarios helps you prepare better for potential surprises throughout the year. If you have to make those decisions in real time, you're less likely to make the best decisions promptly.

4. **"Our marketing plan is accessible to the team at all times for visibility, collaboration, and execution."**

It is common sense that if everyone on the team knows the destination, you are more likely to get there. This becomes even more important in an agile environment, in which things continuously change. If the plan is only visible to some of the team, it is tough to hold the whole team accountable for what they do.

5. **"We have weekly campaign meetings for ideation, strategy, execution, and performance measurement."**

Marketing teams that meet on a regular basis (like sales teams having weekly meetings to review their sales forecast) to review performance versus plan, and make data-driven adjustments, are able to deliver better results over time.

6. **"We have a process in place to adapt our plan in response to unplanned opportunities and strategy changes."**

Plans are not meant to be defined once and rigidly adhered to for a whole year. As real results start flowing in and the world around you changes, the most successful marketing teams create scenarios to model out potential changes to the plan. This could be something internal like being granted more budget or having to make a cut. It could also be something external, like a competitor launching a new product, or a new regulation being announced.

7. **"We regularly measure return on investment on both campaigns and the overall marketing plan."**

The best way to report the value of marketing is through financial metrics that make sense to counterparts outside the marketing function. If you have structured your campaigns appropriately and are measuring at the right level, you will be able to consistently track the relative performance of campaigns in terms of ROI, and understand which campaigns are having the greatest (and the least) impact, with a consistent, comparable metric.

8. **"We can accurately forecast the likelihood of goal achievement throughout the year."**

Some campaigns deliver their results in a rush (e.g., events), others have a spike followed by a long tail (e.g., product launches), yet others deliver consistent metrics, concomitant with investment (e.g., digital advertising for CPG). Modeling out metrics milestones allows you to measure campaign performance thoughtfully throughout the year, and to have better insight into whether you are going to miss, meet, or beat your strategic goals.

Section 2: Budget questions

1. **"We divide up our marketing budget into segments or by function with clear owners for accountability."**

Depending on your team and budget size, it may make sense to cascade budget ownership to individuals on your team, giving them authority to spend in the domains for which they have responsibility. Having monolithic budget ownership and approval normally does not lead to the best marketing outcomes.

2. **"We allocate 60% or more of our budget to campaigns that support our goals."**

People outside of marketing often mistakenly think that the entire marketing budget is allocated toward campaigns. There is normally significant non-campaign investment in things like travel, postage, office supplies and technology. Knowing how much of your budget is dedicated to achieving your strategic campaigns and goals enables you to communicate budget distribution within and outside the team, and it helps you and the team understand whether your investments are well aligned.

3. **"We accurately assign and track all expenses by campaign."**

To generate an accurate ROI, you must be able to track which expenses belong in which campaign. This is not always as simple as it may seem. Digital campaign expenses encompass more than just the media buy. For example, they may include SEO consultants, agencies, copywriters, and more. By capturing 100% of campaign expenses accurately, you can understand the true ROI of your marketing campaigns.

4. **"We have a system for easily identifying and reallocating unused budget."**

Budget underspend is far more common than budget overspend. One of the main culprits behind this is losing track of budget that was planned for a certain campaign or expense but was not fully consumed. It's important to find and roll forward all the unused budget so you can accurately spend 100% of it on time.

5. "We can always see what has been spent and what marketing budget is available."

It seems obvious, but it is difficult to spend with confidence if you don't know what has been spent and what is left. Most companies don't really have an up-to-date view because there is a 4-6 week lag between their spending and receiving the end-of-month close from finance. Maintaining an up-to-date view of 100% of your marketing spend ahead of the monthly finance report allows you to spend with more confidence and avoid under- and over-spend. For example, knowing everything your team has spent on credit cards at a given moment is valuable.

6. "We can accurately report expenses by both marketing campaign and finance budget structure/GL code."

Marketers think in terms of goals, campaigns and metrics. Their finance counterparts normally think in terms of departments, general ledger (GL) codes, and journal entries. These are different languages describing the same budget, and marketing teams need to be able to speak both languages fluently—one to run their marketing plan and budget effectively, and the other to interlock with their colleagues in finance.

7. "We can accurately and efficiently transfer funds across marketing functions as needed."

Plans and budgets set at the beginning of the year inevitably change. To react to such changes, marketers need to be able to efficiently move funds around: to spend less on underperforming or canceled campaigns, and to put funds into the best performing or highest potential campaigns.

8. **"We accurately and quickly reconcile our marketing expenses with finance on a weekly, monthly or quarterly basis."**

With all of the prior points in mind, the finance team is the source of ultimate truth. When the month, quarter and year close, what they say has hit the budget is the only thing anyone pays attention to. So, it's critical that you have a rigorous and effective method of interlocking your understanding of marketing spend with what is in the accounting system, including accruals, reversals, and other accounting entries that might not be intuitive to marketers, but which affect what is left in your budget.

Although this is not an exhaustive list of all the elements of operational excellence in running the marketing function, we know that teams that excel in these areas of plan and budget management will deliver superior results in both absolute and relative terms.

Weighting OMI responses

Despite these being the most critical indicators we identified to measure operational marketing excellence, they are not all equally important. To account for this, we applied weights to specific statements to emphasize their relative levels of importance.

The total contribution of the plan and the budget scores were weighted equally, and converted to scores out of 50 each, resulting in a total score out of 100.

It's important to remember that even with these weights applied, collectively these are the 16 most useful indicators of operational marketing excellence, and every one of them is important.

PLAN WEIGHTING

Heavier
    Our marketing plan is based on a set of measurable goals that align with company objectives

    We create comprehensive campaigns (thematic, integrated, etc.) to execute our strategies and achieve our goals

    We have a process in place to adapt our plan in response to unplanned opportunities and strategy changes

    We regularly measure return on investment on both campaigns and the overall marketing plan

    We do scenario planning so we can quickly react to market dynamics or internal business factors

    Our marketing plan is accessible to the team at all times for visibility, execution, and modification

Lighter
    We can accurately forecast the likelihood of goal achievement throughout the year

    We have weekly campaign meetings for ideation, strategy, execution, and performance measurement

BUDGET WEIGHTING

BUDGET WEIGHTING

Heavier
    We allocate 60% or more of our budget to campaigns that support our goals

    We accurately assign and track all expenses by campaign

    We have a system for easily identifying and reallocating unused budget

    We can always see what has been spent and what marketing budget is available

    We accurately and quickly reconcile our marketing expenses with finance on a weekly, monthly or quarterly basis

    We divide up our marketing budget into segments or by function with clear owners for accountability

    We can accurately and efficiently transfer funds across marketing functions as needed

Lighter
    We can accurately report expenses by both marketing campaign and finance budget structure/GL code

Finally, the sample size for these results is 217. Now onto the results:

OMI survey results

Here is a high-level summary of the results overall:

	MEAN	MEDIAN	MIN	MAX
PLAN	43%	40%	0%	92%
BUDGET	46%	45%	0%	100%
TOTAL	**45%**	**44%**	**4%**	**92%**

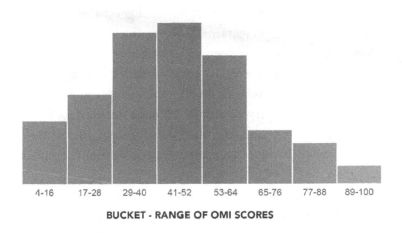

BUCKET - RANGE OF OMI SCORES

The mean OMI score is 45 and the median is 44. It's not quite a normal distribution, with a longer tail to the right, meaning scores are concentrated below the average. Most respondents are to the left of the middle column. 62% of respondents had an OMI below 50.

The following line graph is another way of seeing the distribution that illustrates how a small majority of answers fall below the mean of 45.

In general, the fairly low score totals suggest that the state of operational marketing presents many opportunities for improvement.

Next, we look one layer deeper and look at the Budget and Plan scores separately. This allows us to see where the largest gaps exist, and the impact of our weighting on the overall scores.

Below is a summary of results by each statement. We have grouped the top two and bottom two responses into categories marked "Good/Fair" and "Poor/None" in order to make the chart more legible.

It's easy to see that most respondents score themselves in the "Poor/None" category versus the "Good/Fair" category for nearly all the questions. If you feel you could improve your operational marketing excellence, you are not alone. In the subsequent sections we explore the planning and budgeting responses in more detail.

OMI Results for Marketing Planning

The table below summarizes the responses to the individual budget statements into top-two box responses. First, we generalized the responses to approximate the meaning of "we do this well" (positive) and "we don't do this well" (negative). The light bars indicate the statements that garnered positive answers from >50% of respondents. The dark-shaded bars indicate statements that amassed positive answers from <50% of respondents.

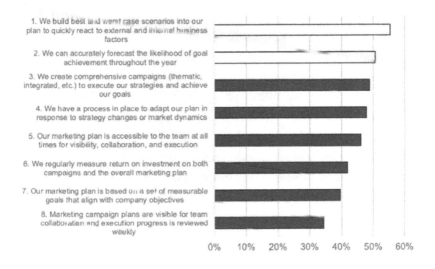

Mixed messages on goals

Statement 1("We build best and worst case scenarios into our plan to quickly react to external and internal business factors") indicates that the majority of the sampled population is considering areas they would adjust as changes come into play, as a planning step. An example of an internal factor might be a required budget cut. An external factor might be a new market dynamic, like a new regulation.

Note that the relative confidence level in these responses is somewhat at odds with the responses to Statement 4 ("We have a process in place to adapt our plan in response to strategy changes or market dynamics). This would seem to indicate that the scenario analysis is a more static process that is done episodically (e.g., "What will we do with our Facebook investments if Apple changes its application permissions model?") than an agile one (e.g., "We regularly meet to discuss what changes, if any, we should make to the plan based on our current assessment of internal and external factors and our latest campaign performance data"). The former is more akin to creating plans B, C and D; the latter is data-driven adaptation. Both are important.

Statement 2 ("We can accurately forecast the likelihood of goal achievement throughout the year)" is the other question yielding top-2 responses above 50%. This is a little perplexing given the low score of Statement 7 ("Our marketing plan is based on a set of measurable goals that align with company objectives.") **Less than 40%** of respondents say they do goals-based planning aligned with corporate objectives well—yet, **more than 50%** of respondents say they can forecast their goals accurately.

Based on the goals and plans we've analyzed, we believe that the delta lies in the goal-setting process itself. A marketing team may set a goal of achieving two million website visits in a year. This is very measurable, and it should be fairly easy to predict whether that goal will be achieved.

It is also possible that this goal may not be aligned with the company strategy and the company's goals. Misaligned goals are likely to cause frustration for everyone. The marketing team works hard, achieves the goal of two million site visits, celebrates it, and their counterparts outside marketing say, "So what? How's that helpful?" This is demoralizing for the marketing team that's worked so hard to achieve something no one seems to care about. It's also difficult to prove value if your key outcomes seem esoteric or peripheral to your non-marketing colleagues. On the other hand, if marketing's goals are well aligned with corporate goals, then marketing's victories are the company's victories.

An area for future study is to look at how marketing's goals are selected, especially if they're not in alignment with company goals.

There's a significant opportunity to enhance data sharing and collaboration

54% of respondents say their marketing plan's visibility to the entire team is inadequate or non-existent. 65% say the same of their campaign plans and reviews. With increasing geographic diversity, remote working, and international team composition, there is tremendous opportunity in enhancing visibility and collaboration. If Team A does not know what Team B is doing, and neither team has access to the plan, what are some potential consequences?

- Both teams are likely to carry out well-intentioned, but non-strategic, marketing activities. If they can't see the plan and the goals, they don't know where to aim, damaging overall MROI for the plan
- Teams A and B may duplicate each other's efforts
- Team A's efforts may clash with, or even undermine, Team B's efforts
- Team A and Team B may make discrete investments in things like agencies or technology that they could have negotiated more effectively together

As has already happened in most other business functions, marketing should consolidate and centralize its plans into a single system of record, and then ensure that the plan and the budget are completely visible to all team members.

There is a gap between planning and execution

Three of the top four results (Statements 1, 3 and 4) relate to process and planning. Three of the four bottom results (5, 6, and 8) relate to execution. Plans have little value if they can't be executed.

There are highly actionable, simple steps that companies can take to close this gap:

- Create a shared, centralized, single data record that the whole team works on
- Set permissions appropriately; not everyone should have access to everything
- Meet frequently to review data and progress, and then adjust accordingly. Sales teams meet weekly to review progress, but most marketing teams do not have a regular cadence of meetings to do the same. This isn't surprising given the fact that the data needed for such a review typically lives in a dozen disparate silos. Big gaps between reviews means missed opportunities to double down on over-performing campaigns, and pulling the plug on underperforming ones.

Budget Results

As with the planning results, it is noteworthy that the industry does not highly rate its operational excellence for budget management. Only two questions secured top two responses over 50%, and no overwhelming strengths emerged.

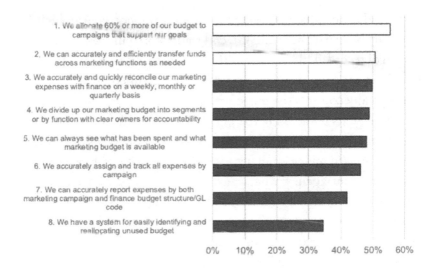

1. We allocate 60% or more of our budget to campaigns that support our goals

2. We can accurately and efficiently transfer funds across marketing functions as needed

3. We accurately and quickly reconcile our marketing expenses with finance on a weekly, monthly or quarterly basis

4. We divide up our marketing budget into segments or by function with clear owners for accountability

5. We can always see what has been spent and what marketing budget is available

6. We accurately assign and track all expenses by campaign

7. We can accurately report expenses by both marketing campaign and finance budget structure/GL code

8. We have a system for easily identifying and reallocating unused budget

0%   10%   20%   30%   40%   50%   60%

More mixed messages on goal setting

55% of respondents report strong performance in allocating >60% of their budget to campaigns that support their goals. On the other hand, as we saw in the planning results, only 40% report they do well in setting goals that are aligned with company objectives. This seems to support the notion that teams may be setting marketing goals that are not aligned with company objectives. While it is encouraging that campaign investments are successfully aligned with goals, it's important to ensure those marketing goals tie to company objectives.

There is confusion about what has been spent and what is available

The four lowest scores (Statements 5 through 8) indicate that many marketing teams are struggling to keep accurate track of their expenses, in a variety of ways. The data shows that marketers find assigning expenses to campaigns accurately to be a challenge. This makes it impossible to calculate campaign ROI. They struggle to map their campaign-oriented view to a finance view, which is normally by department and GL code, and stored in the accounting system of record. This makes it difficult to discuss where investments have been made, and which investments are planned, with the team that actually controls the purse strings.

Statements 5 and 8 are the biggest causes of the most common budget challenge we observe: underspend. Because teams can't easily identify unused budget, and because they can't accurately track what has been spent against what is available, it's difficult for them to spend with confidence. Underspend is the most pervasive financial challenge marketers face. By establishing systems and processes to accurately assign expenses to campaigns, tracking what has been spent/what remains, and being able to nimbly re-assign budget, marketing teams can ensure they spend 100% of their budget on strategically-aligned activities.

The operational excellence gap: contrasting highest and lowest operational excellence

In the charts below, we show the difference between the strongest responses ("We excel at this.") and the weakest responses ("We don't do this at all.") by statement. Specifically, we deducted the percentage of responses in the lowest category ("We don't do this at all.") from the percentage of scores in the strongest category ("We excel at this."), for each question in the survey.

We use this to highlight the spread between the strongest and weakest self-assessments in each of the statements in the survey. If the weakest responses strongly outnumber the strongest, that indicates that the population is not performing well in this critical area of operational marketing excellence. If the strongest scores outweigh the weakest ones, it suggests that confidence is higher.

Budget Results

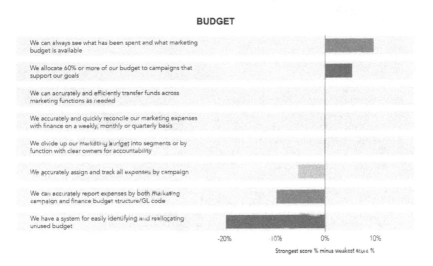

BUDGET

We can always see what has been spent and what marketing budget is available

We allocate 60% or more of our budget to campaigns that support our goals

We can accurately and efficiently transfer funds across marketing functions as needed

We accurately and quickly reconcile our marketing expenses with finance on a weekly, monthly or quarterly basis

We divide up our marketing budget into segments or by function with clear owners for accountability

We accurately assign and track all expenses by campaign

We can accurately report expenses by both marketing campaign and finance budget structure/GL code

We have a system for easily identifying and reallocating unused budget

-20%   -10%   0%   10%

Strongest score % minus weakest score %

This ranking follows that of the top-two budget charts above, but by only including the highest and lowest ratings, we can better see the overall skew, which is clearly towards operational weaknesses in marketing budget management.

There is no overwhelmingly strong category. The biggest challenges surround understanding what budget is available, and assigning investment accurately to campaigns. The consequence? Usually chronic underspend. Responsible marketing leaders don't want to exceed their budgets, but poor visibility and spend tracking, coupled with poor alignment with finance, leads to an inability to confidently spend 100% of the budget on time, and on the right things.

Plan Results

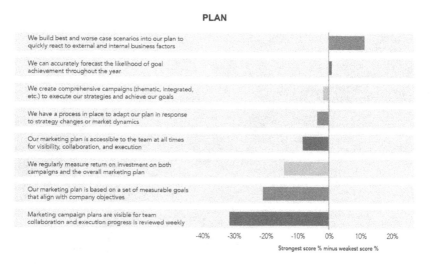

When it comes to planning, the highly negative responses outweigh the highly positive ones. Creating marketing goals that are aligned with corporate objectives is a serious weakness, as is plan execution.

The term "plan execution" does not mean campaign or tactic execution (e.g., writing content, producing video, SEO, etc.). Rather, it is the implementation, measurement, and tuning of the plan and budget to achieve the plan objectives. Tactics may be executed at a world-class level, but if they don't yield campaign results that add up to meaningful business value, they're all for nothing. Worse, if the team does not have a culture of operational excellence, it may work hard throughout the year, delivering high-quality tactics but low-quality outcomes.

Correlates of success

Next, let's look at the characteristics of the companies who scored highest on the OMI, indicating the respondents with the highest degree of operational excellence in marketing. Analyzing their scores in more depth helps to uncover a path for other companies that are striving to improve their marketing performance.

We created another histogram from the survey results, reducing the number of buckets to just four. This gives us four cohorts for comparison.

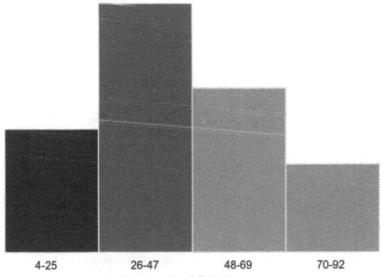

| 4-25 | 26-47 | 48-69 | 70-92 |

Histogram of OMI Scores

The numbers beneath each column indicate the range of scores captured in each bucket. We now have four cohorts of respondents, representing the highest, second, third, and lowest scores respectively. We wanted to explore whether the top-performing companies were consistently good at specific skills covered in the survey.

In the following charts, we compare scores by question between the cohorts. To make the charts legible, we have not mapped the entire list of questions into the x-axis. Rather, we have used a name that can be referenced to look up the specific question. Here is the mapping of names to questions:

Budget Q1   We divide up our marketing budget into segments or by function with clear owners for accountability

Budget Q2   We allocate 60% or more of our budget to campaigns that support our goals

Budget Q3   We accurately assign and track all expenses by campaign

Budget Q4   We have a system for easily identifying and reallocating unused budget

Budget Q5   We can always see what has been spent and what marketing budget is available

Budget Q6   We can accurately report expenses by both marketing campaign and finance budget structure/GL code

Budget Q7   We can accurately and efficiently transfer funds across marketing functions as needed

Budget Q8   We accurately and quickly reconcile our marketing expenses with finance on a weekly, monthly or quarterly basis

Plan Q1   Our marketing plan is based on a set of measurable goals that align with company objectives

Plan Q2   We create comprehensive campaigns (thematic, integrated, etc.) to execute our strategies and achieve our goals

Plan Q3   We do scenario planning so we can quickly react to market dynamics or internal business factors

Plan Q4   Our marketing plan is accessible to the team at all times for visibility, execution, and modification

Plan Q5   We have weekly campaign meetings for ideation, strategy, execution, and performance measurement

Plan Q6   We have a process in place to adapt our plan in response to unplanned opportunities and strategy changes

Plan Q7   We regularly measure return on investment on both campaigns and the overall marketing plan

Plan Q8   We can accurately forecast the likelihood of goal achievement throughout the year

The chart below compares the median score per statement for the highest-scoring cohort versus the second highest-scoring cohort. The top-performing cohort is represented by the black dots, and the second-best cohort by the white squares.

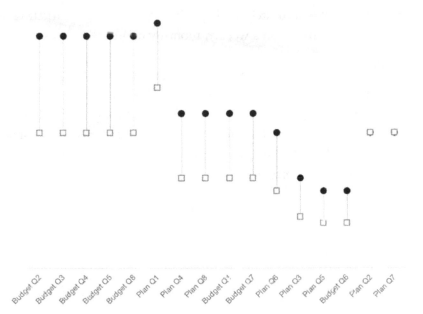

The immediately striking observation is that the main separation between the top-performing cohort and the second cohort is budgetary excellence. While using a goals-based planning approach (Plan Q1) is the single highest-impact statement, the gap between top-performing companies and the next cohort is driven mainly by the budget management topics. These key budgetary topics are:

Budget Q2: We allocate 60% or more of our budget to campaigns that support our goals
Budget Q3: We accurately assign and track all expenses by campaign
Budget Q4: We have a system for easily identifying and reallocating unused budget
Budget Q5: We can always see what has been spent and what marketing budget is available
Budget Q6: We can accurately report expenses by both marketing campaign and finance budget structure/GL code

Budget Q8: We accurately and quickly reconcile our marketing expenses with finance on a weekly, monthly or quarterly basis

The discovery that budgetary questions drive the largest gap between the top two cohorts led us to examine the relative impacts of plan versus budget performance across all four cohorts. The chart below compares the median budget scores (i.e., the median of the sub-total of all budget questions) and the median plan scores for each of the four cohorts.

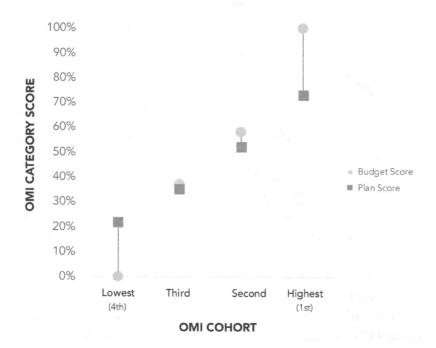

Both plan and budget scores increase as we move up through the cohorts, meaning that teams improve both planning and budgeting excellence. It is readily apparent that the rate of increase in budgeting excellence outstrips that of planning, and that top-performing teams score higher in budgetary excellence than they do in planning.

There is practically no difference between the two categories in the third cohort, and a large difference in the lowest, where companies are reporting significant deficiencies in managing their budgets effectively.

Finally, we decided to look at OMI scores by cohort in one more way. We split the questions into categories that mixed planning and budgeting questions together and differentiated on two new factors: creation and implementation. A subset of the statements in the OMI survey queried how marketing teams set up their plans and budgets. These fall into the category of creation. The other questions probe how marketers implement their plans and budgets. These fall into the category of implementation. Note that questions that refer to having systems or processes in place fall into the creation category, because they do not cover whether those systems are effectively used. The split is as follows:

Creation

We divide up our marketing budget into segments or by function with clear owners for accountability

We allocate 60% or more of our budget to campaigns that support our goals

We have a system for easily identifying and reallocating unused budget

Our marketing plan is based on a set of measurable goals that align with company objectives

We create comprehensive campaigns (thematic, integrated, etc.) to execute our strategies and achieve our goals

We have a process in place to adapt our plan in response to unplanned opportunities and strategy changes

Implementation

We accurately assign and track all expenses by campaign

We can always see what has been spent and what marketing budget is available

We can accurately report expenses by both marketing
campaign and finance budget structure/GL code

We can accurately and efficiently transfer funds
across marketing functions as needed

We accurately and quickly reconcile our marketing expenses
with finance on a weekly, monthly or quarterly basis

We do scenario planning so we can quickly react to
market dynamics or internal business factors

Our marketing plan is accessible to the team at all times
for visibility, execution, and modification

We have weekly campaign meetings for ideation, strategy,
execution, and performance measurement

We regularly measure return on investment on both
campaigns and the overall marketing plan

We can accurately forecast the likelihood of goal
achievement throughout the year

We calculated performance by cohort along these two
dimensions, as a percentage of the total possible score. The results
are shown below:

100%			
90%			
80%			
70%			
60%			
50%			
40%			
30%			
20%			
10%			
0%			
Highest	Second	Third	Lowest

■ Creation ▨ Implementation

The lowest performing companies have weaker plan and budget creation scores, but significantly lower implementation. By contrast, the higher performing companies not only have much better plan and budget creation scores, they excel at implementation as well.

OMI conclusions

There are significant opportunities to enhance operational marketing excellence as measured by the OMI. 100% of companies report that they could improve their marketing operational excellence, and more than 90% report that they have substantial opportunities to improve.

As a whole, the survey indicates that marketing teams face more challenges implementing plans and budgets than in creating them. This is particularly notable in spend management, with companies reporting difficulties in tracking expenses by GL code and campaign, and struggling to understand what has been spent and what is left.

This spend management challenge hinders the ability to calculate ROI accurately, which in turn makes it difficult to adjust the plan to optimize the highest performing programs. It also leads to chronic underspend, which is by far the most common budget management challenge marketing teams face.

Execution is the single biggest weakness in marketing planning as well. Most companies report poor plan visibility and low collaboration. Teams living with poor visibility are more likely to spend resources on non-strategic activities, and less likely to achieve successful outcomes.

Even though plan creation scores are generally better than plan implementation scores, it is notable that only 39% of plans are based on strategic goals aligned with corporate goals. Hopefully it is clear at this stage in the book that we are strong proponents of goals-based planning. We would recommend that every company prioritize setting clear goals that are aligned with company objectives.

The survey responses also indicate that some marketing teams may be working toward goals that are not aligned with company goals. This is likely to cause frustration both inside and outside the marketing team, because despite lots of hard work, there is a reasonable probability the company will not value marketing outcomes that aren't oriented toward company objectives.

There are three distinctive characteristics of the highest performing cohort, besides the obvious fact of getting higher aggregate scores.:

1. **Goals-based planning:** The top-performing companies consistently scored highest in developing goals-based plans, aligned with company goals. 97% of the top cohort reported excellent or good goals-based planning versus 76% (2nd cohort), 51% (3rd cohort) and 16% (lowest cohort).

2. **Financial management:** For the respondents with the highest OMI scores, their budget scores were generally even

higher than their planning scores. By contrast, the bottom cohort had very poor budget scores. It is imperative for teams to have a strong handle on their budget so they can measure ROI, report accurately, spend confidently, and use 100% of their budget on strategic activities. If the spend is uncertain, everything is uncertain.

3. **Implementation:** Marketing teams with the highest OMI scores achieved excellent results in topics related to implementing the plans they created. In fact, their implementation scored even higher than their plan creation scores. By contrast, lower-scoring companies performed better in creating their plans and budgets than in implementing them.

When a plan and budget have been created, it is good practice to pause and answer the question, "How are we going to do this?" Perhaps some more hiring, outsourcing, or tech is needed to deliver the plan. By addressing the question of how in addition to the question of what, marketers will increase their chances of achieving their goals.

APPENDIX

OMI Survey - all results

The following series of charts shows results for each question. The charts are ordered from the highest proportion of most positive responses to the lowest across both planning and budgeting questions.

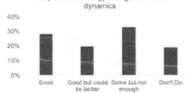

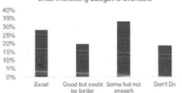

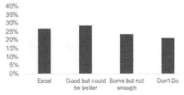

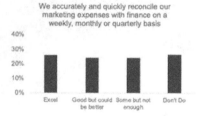

We accurately and quickly reconcile our marketing expenses with finance on a weekly, monthly or quarterly basis

We can accurately forecast the likelihood of goal achievement throughout the year

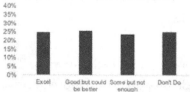

We can accurately and efficiently transfer funds across marketing functions as needed

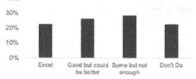

We create comprehensive campaigns (thematic, integrated, etc.) to execute our strategies and achieve our goals

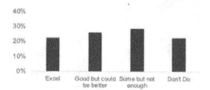

We divide up our marketing budget into segments or by function with clear owners for accountability

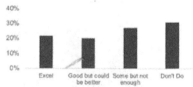

We regularly measure return on investment on both campaigns and the overall marketing plan

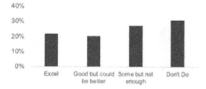

We can accurately report expenses by both marketing campaign and finance budget structure/GL code

Our marketing plan is accessible to the team at all times for visibility, collaboration, and execution

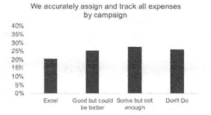

We accurately assign and track all expenses by campaign

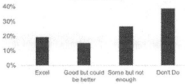

Marketing campaign plans are visible for team collaboration and execution progress is reviewed weekly

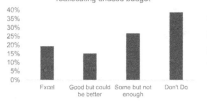

We have a system for easily identifying and reallocating unused budget

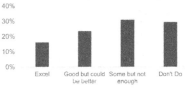

Our marketing plan is based on a set of measurable goals that align with company objectives

231

CONCLUSION

Congratulations! You made it through a lot of content, representing over 70 years of combined experience in marketing leadership. If you made it this far, you are the kind of leader who is committed to learning and improving your craft.

You learned about the challenges facing marketing leaders and the costs of not addressing those problems. More importantly, you now understand how to build a framework for operational excellence in your marketing organization, combined with a specific set of best practices including goals-based marketing planning, building a winning marketing plan, designing campaigns to achieve your goals, managing a marketing budget, and much more.

While you've reached the end of the book, we hope this is the beginning of a relationship with The Next CMO community. In the appendix, you will find some helpful tools and templates to facilitate the implementation of these practices. You can also find digital versions of these templates, along with many more useful resources, at TheNextCMO.com.

We hope to see you there soon.

TEMPLATES AND EXHIBITS

Marketing Plan template

Plan Element	Plan Contents
Situation analysis	
Market research & analysis	
Company goals	
Marketing goals	
Marketing strategies	
Target audience (including segmentation)	
Positioning and messaging	
Product and services direction & definition	
Pricing and packaging	
Competitive analysis	
Sales channel strategy	
Sales support	
Partner/channel strategy	
Product and services launches	
Campaigns	
Marketing channels (vehicles)	
Programs	
Marketing activity timeline	

Team structure, growth and responsibilities	
Technology (software)	
Budget allocation	
Testing	
Metrics of achievement	
Assumptions, dependencies, risks	

Marketing strategy template

Strategy Template	(determining if the strategy is the right fit)
Goal	Goal detail
Proposed strategy	Choose a strategy to achieve the goal
Factors	**Determining strategy viability**
Team	Evaluate the team (experienced, average, junior)
Budget	Estimate the budget (high, medium, low)
Complexity	Determine the complexity (high, medium, low)
Target audience	Define the audience (prospect, customer, partner, press, etc.)
Competition	Research the competition (differentiation, pricing, etc.)
Industry	Learn the industry (regulated vs. unregulated)
Region	Discover the region (cultural differences, regulations, holidays, etc.)
Product/service fit	Define the product or service (complex vs. simple)
Timeline	Estimate the time it will take to execute (base it on the goal timeline)
Historical data	Analyze the data (level of achievement, room for improvement)
Expected ROI	Calculate the potential ROI (revenue, contribution margin)

Campaign template

Campaign Name	
Goals	
Audience	
Topline Message	
Supporting Messages	
Marketing Strategy	
Call To Action	
Success Metrics	
Campaign Duration	
Content	
Marketing Channels	
Nurturing Activity	
Internal Communications	
Timeline	
Budget	
Expected ROI	

465662050R00105